In memory to those who have given their lives
in the name of peace.

Foreword

William Neilson Brown was born on the 3rd May, 1883, into a Scottish Borders family of textile mill owners. His father, Alexander Laing Brown was the MP for the Border Burghs during the 1880's.

At the age of 17, Brown joined the local Volunteers and then the Border Rifle Volunteers, winning several shooting prizes at Bisley, before joining the 4th Battalion King's Own Scottish Borderers. He served as a volunteer from 1900 – 1908.

When the 1st World War broke out in 1914, he volunteered for service with the Army Service Corps in Japan, before returning home and joining the 2nd Battalion, Gordon Highlanders in 1915.

During his service, Major Brown was wounded twice; In October 1917 and January 1918, and won the Military Cross for gallantry and bravery in Italy, Belgium and France, as well as the 1914 Star, British War Medal, Allied Victory Medal and the Italian Generals Silver Medal for the Battle of Piave.

Normally, letters written in the field would be censored, however, the letters which you are about to read are particularly graphic and extraordinarily detailed, whilst laced with his wry humour and wisdom.

The letters were written between 1915 – 1918 from both France and Italy to his Aunt, Minnie McGillivray, who lived in Galashiels, in the Scottish Borders.

There are over 40 letters, reproduced as they were written, from the hell of the trenches to tucking into a delightful, although unexpected meal on Christmas Day – these are some of the most colourful, graphic and moving accounts of a soldier's life during World War 1.

William had always had a literary leaning both before and after the Great War. He was a published author and at one time was editor of the 'Border Standard', now the 'Border Telegraph'. You will see by his letters his undoubted flair for writing.

Perhaps this passion for the written word came from his uncle, James Brown, better known as J.B. Selkirk, the Scottish poet.

After the war William Brown travelled extensively before returning to the Borders, where he met and married Marjorie Isabella MacGowan. They had two children, William Alexander Brown, who passed away in 1984 and a daughter, Margery, who at the time of compiling this book, resides in Melbourne, Australia.

During the Second World War he was engaged in the censorship division of the Admiralty which was stationed at Scapa Flow.

His son William Alexander Brown followed his father into the army; Argyll and Sutherland Highlanders, also attaining the rank of major and was awarded the MBE as well as Pakistan's highest military honour for securing the Gilgit province for Pakistan during the partition of India in 1947.

William Neilson Brown died, age 70, in August 1953 and is buried with his wife, who survived him by 30 years, in Wairds cemetery, Melrose, Scottish Borders.

Medals from left to right:
Military Cross, 1914 ASC V Star, 1914-1918 British War Medal,
Allied Victory Medal, Italian Generals Silver Medal

Locations of the 2nd Battalion, Gordon Highlanders
August 1916 to February 1919

August 1916   Picquiney, Buire

September 1916   Mametz, Airaines, La Creche, Pont de Nieppe

October 1916   Pont de Nieppe, Lebezet

November 1916   Doullens, Bertrancourt, Beaumont Hamel

December 1916   Bertrancourt, Beaumont Hamel

January-March 1917   Bertrancourt, Beaumont Hamel, Louvencourt, Beauval, Mailly – Mallet

April 1917   La Mairie de Behagnies, Courcelles - le – Comte

May-July 1917   Bullecourt, Gommecourt, Ecoust - Saint – Mein

August 1917   Ervillers, Bailleulmont, Poperinghe

September 1917   Steenvoorde, Hondeghen, Salperwick, Renninghelst

October 1917   Dickebush, Zillebeke, Gheluvelt, Kemmel, Blaringhem

November 1917   Blaringhem, Remilly Wirquin, Blangy sur Ternoise, Wavrans, then by rail to Italy

December 1917   Curtarolo, Loreggia, Brusaporco, Riese - Pio, Villa ca Amata

January 1918   Villa ca Amata, Cuisignana, Nervesa

February 1918   Bavaria, Cusignana

March 1918   Vedelago, Campodoro, Grumalo, Bolzano, Sarcedo

April 1918   Mount Pau, Mount Lemerle

May 1918   Asiago Plateau, Carriola, Mount Pau, Mt Serona, Mount Brusabo, San Dona di Piave

June 1918   Arzignano, Santa Maria, Brusabo

July 1918   Brusabo, Mount Pau, Mt Serona, Cavalletto, Montecchio – Maggiore

September 1918   Montecchio – Maggiore

October 1918   Montecchio - Maggiore, Marano, Treviso, Grave di Papadopoli, Casa Nerdi

November 1918   Gradisca, Arzenutto, Godega - di - Sant - Urbano, Campolungo

December 1918   Campolungo, Sossano

January 1919   Sossano

February 1919   Sossano, Lonigo, Montecchio – Maggiore

March 1919   Turin, Genoa - by rail - Le Havre, Southampton (23rdMarch), Aberdeen (24th March).

Locations in France

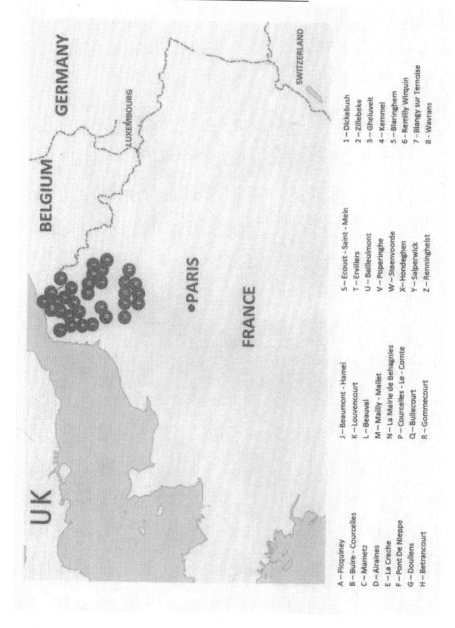

A – Picquigny
B – Buire - Courcelles
C – Mametz
D – Airaines
E – La Creche
F – Pont De Nieppe
G – Doullens
H – Betrancourt

J – Beaumont - Hamel
K – Louvencourt
L – Beauval
M – Mailly - Maillet
N – La Mairie de Behagnies
P – Courcelles - Le - Comte
Q – Bullecourt
R – Gommecourt

S – Ecoust - Saint - Mein
T – Ervillers
U – Bailleulmont
V – Poperinghe
W – Steenvoorde
X – Hondeghem
Y – Salperwick
Z – Renninghelst

1 - Dickiebush
2 - Zillebeke
3 - Ghelluvelt
4 - Kemmel
5 - Blaringhem
6 - Remilly Wirquin
7 - Blangy sur Ternoise
8 - Wavrans

Locations in Italy

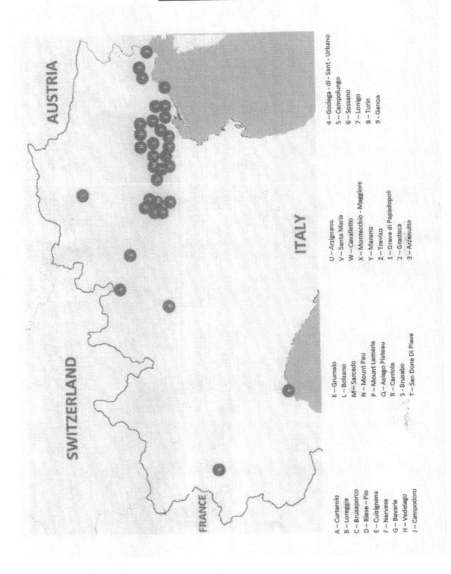

AUSTRIA

SWITZERLAND

FRANCE

ITALY

A – Curtarolo
B – Loreggia
C – Brussaporco
D – Riese – Pio
E – Cuisignana
F – Nervesa
G – Bavaria
H – Vedelago
J – Campodoro

K – Grumolo
L – Bolzano
M – Sarcedo
N – Mount Pau
P – Mount Lemerle
Q – Asiago Plateau
R – Carriola
S – Brusabo
T – San Dona Di Piave

U – Arzignano
V – Santa Maria
W – Cavalletto
X – Montecchio - Maggiore
Y – Marano
Z – Treviso
1 – Grave di Papadopoli
2 – Gradisca
3 – Arzenutto

4 – Godega - di - Sant - Urbano
5 – Campolungo
6 – Sossano
7 – Lonigo
8 – Turin
9 – Genoa

Letters 1 – 13 were written when William Brown was a volunteer with the Army Service Corps

****

Letter 1

ASC France

The parcels are arriving all right and are very welcome. The only thing you might send me is a pipe, I have only one left and it would be awful to be left without one. Things jog on from day to day. I can never get used to the shells. I don't mind saying they are awful especially at night. We are in France now and in a splendid part of the country, very like the Borders. We are resting now after a terrific fight in which our division held two army corps at bay for four days. But at an awful cost about 60% of our strength. We hear plenty of tales but get no news except from the English newspapers, and laugh at the accounts of the fight we were in. The country here is a welcome change from the desolation of Belgium. It would break your heart to see the houses and churches smashed and empty. The old world architecture burned and destroyed just like our border abbeys. I have not got a scratch yet but the thing is just starting. The German prisoners are a different lot a poor class of men, weary and hungry but they have the iron discipline which carries them through without a falter. The accuracy with which they shell a town is a revelation, and it is very unpleasant as the place where the troops are come in for special attention I have gone through two horses now and am in the saddle so this keeps me fit and well. We have some very dangerous work at nights, galloping up and down the convoys, and one night my horse fell just as a shell burst right in front. He was done and lay still and I thought both he and I were hit. The horse I have just now is a very good one I found it after one of the regiments had been cut up. He is rather light however and won't last long. I met a clergyman the other night and we had a long argument on *pre destination*, with the guns roaring all around. The roads are full of all kind of transport and the mud is inches and feet deep. Good luck to you all.

pre destination – Does God decide the outcome?

****

****

Letter 2

ASC France

I had a night out lately. We started at 6pm loaded up with food and then made our way to the trenches. Of course we had guides. It was snowing and fairly warm and I enjoyed the journey as the road was well known. When we got up we halted behind a farm and brought the wagons up one by one to a deserted farm house and unloaded as quickly as possible. All the time the bullets came zip zip over our heads and it took two hours to unload it was very exciting. This is the first time I have been under rifle fire and you can't help ducking though it is so ridiculous as the bullet is passed you before you can move. When a bullet struck the road there was a flash of fire from the flints from which the roads are made. There was one little stretch of about thirty yards that we had to cross openly and it was rather nasty to hear the bullets thudding in the soft earth at the back. Add to the difficulties the place that we had to turn in was very narrow, but everything came off alright, no one was hit and only one bullet hole through my wagon. The night was so still that the Germans could hear us and this is probably what drew the fire, I got back at 4am next morning. Some days are very cold but it changes very unpleasantly and some days are too warm.

****

Photo of regiment before going off to war

****

Letter 3

No more news of any kind. We are having some fighting but not much. The snipers are busy and are very dangerous. I had to take a wagon of braziers up to the trenches to warm up the men. It was a perfect night, keen hard frost. A full moon lit up the white field and the roads echoed with the rumble of the wagon. We passed a little group on the roadside talking about football and smoking their pipes. In the middle one lay on a stretcher with no overcoat on. We knew what that meant but one gets used to that here. A man in front of us got his hand hit with a spent bullet but it broke two of his fingers. We had it dressed and took him in with us, seven miles in the awful cold in a wagon I was very glad to get back from the trenches which are in a big horseshoe, and this makes it much more dangerous as you never know how near you are to the actual fighting line. There the best shots of both armies lie and wait for the slightest movement. When we were digging in the garden of our house today we came on over a thousand pounds of bonds and a great quantity of silver. If it had been Germany it would have been alright, but we had to find the owner, an old woman. The cold has been awful but it has broken today and now the mud is up to our ears. We have magnificent sunsets, real *Millet* pictures. A great flaming background of scarlet with the low flat landscape, broken only by the church spires, and long lines of poplars straight into the sinking sun. The horses are difficult to manage, two have died of pneumonia and a skin disease has broken out among them, but it is nothing serious. I have forty in my command and this takes a lot of looking after. We have no change in the food but chickens at five francs a pair the price fixed by the authorities and the bacon and bully beef get very monotonous. We get some fresh meat occasionally and make good stews with fresh vegetables. This place is very comfortable but we expect to get shelled out any day. After our last experience this shall not be so cheery. You will see in the papers about the destruction of Ypres. We came out after it was smashed and burning. The people we stayed with were awfully nice but they would be killed. Two women and three little children. They were very kind to me and it is awful to think that the house that withstood the first week of the bombardment when I was in it should be an empty shell and the inmates dead and gone.

Millet – French artist

****

Letter 4

ASC France

All well yet and very quiet. I have got the parcels and they are very welcome. The cold is awful now and if you could send some mufflers for the men I would be very glad. I am fairly comfortable just now. There is not so much to do now that I have got the company but there is a great deal more responsibility. I have seen about the whole of Flanders now and as we never stay longer than a few days in one place you can understand that France has become very well known to me. It is strange to think that for fourteen months we have never been more than four miles from the firing line and the guns have become such an every day thing that no one notices them. The whole house shakes when the big ones go off. You would laugh, though it is a shame to see the people flying into the cellars when a big shell comes in. The woman snatch up the children and the men bang up the shutters and fly after them. Then when the 'straffing' is over everything just goes on as usual and in half an hour it is forgotten. Casualties in these affairs are astonishingly small. The wind is the awful thing here it pierces through and through on the long plains the sunsets are magnificent and it is so clear that you can see churches miles away rising above the long lines of poplars. I am just going to give the men a rum issue no teetotallers here everyone joins in the rum even the sons of temperance, anyone who tried to stop the rum here would get into trouble.

****

William Neilson Brown

Letter 5

ASC France

All well. We are in it again but not with the same vigour. The worst of the battle seems to be over and the Germans have had fearful losses. Ours have been very heavy and we cannot afford to lose men. The trenches are quiet except for a little artillery fire and the snipers who kill a few on both sides every day. We have frost now and bitter winds but we are very comfortable in a deserted village. Many of the houses are smashed but the church is the worst. It was shelled and destroyed by fire and must have been a magnificent building. The Germans had machine guns on the tower so the French had to smash it. We are very far from being without news here as we get yesterdays paper every day from the motor transport so keep in touch with what is going on. The men are very well fed and clothes are good and wintering will not be so bad in fact if a hard frost came the roads would improve for they are a sea of mud six and eight inches deep. If you can get any mufflers or socks from your different associations send them for my men as the ASC do not get much and it is cold work driving in all kinds of weather. I'll tell you what you might send, a box of kippers or two boxes, as for the bacon eternal bacon has become awful. We expect to be in this place for a long time so will get them alright. The troops are very comfortable in the trenches. We have given them plenty of straw and coke to make fires and they have candles so they can play cards and write in the intervals between killing Germans. All the French guns here have names on them 'The Innocent' 'Lady Caprice' 'The Maiden' etc. and I had five shots the other day with one of them. I was staying with the captain in a barn and he could speak some English. He insisted on my firing for luck so I pulled the string after the gun had been laid. Five shots were plenty as it gives you an awful headache if you are not used to it. This is the only chance I have had of killing Germans, and this is the worst of our work, we have to take such risks and never get a shot back. I have had to shoot a lot of horses and this is all the use I have put it to. All the women were bundled out of here yesterday as we are expecting another battle to begin, and I took them in my wagons for about five miles and then set them off, God knows where. It is very sad as they hate leaving their homes even when they are smashed. They did not appear very cast down but the little children suffer from the cold. My new horse is lasting well but you never can count on their health when much night work is done.

****

Letter 6

ASC France Christmas 1915

All well. Very cold now, hard frost and sleet. I spent Christmas Eve on a wagon on special duty. A straw bed but very comfortable. All night the rifles were pattering away, sniping is in full swing and every now and again a big gun roared in the distance. The maxims hammered away at intervals, and the men were singing hymns with great gusto, there was an extra dose of rum issued and it was funny to think of the contrasts. It was a glorious night, the trees, tall straight poplars, and the church towers stood out in the moonlight. We had a fine dinner on Christmas day in a comfortable house. The house is fine with only one shell hole in it up in the attics, so the rain does not get in. 'The menu' was, ox soup, sardines, roast chicken, welsh rarebit, plum pudding, figs, dates, apples chocolates, sweets. Wines, burgundy, port, coffee and brandy 1815 and rum and hot water to finish off with. Fine cigars and cigarettes made the evening just perfect. Old 'Kaiser' the *coy* goose unfortunately got run over by a motor lorry during his morning stroll and was so flat that he had to be accorded a military funeral. I think it was rather a relief to all parties as we could hardly have killed him and he was a nuisance to cart about. We have a horse in the coy that is beloved by all. He was born tired and lies down whenever we have a halt on the road this enrages his driver who has to groom him, and provides amusement for all. He takes his breakfast in bed every morning refusing to get up and eats his hay with a quiet dignity which disarms his driver armed with a big whip. The horses have suffered a good deal with the wet but they are all well fed and have good rugs. I had a photo taken in a ruined church but it did not come out. It is strange to see a church ruined and a dreadful figure of Christ unharmed on the wall. The churches have had a bad time as the spires make good places for machine guns. The churchyards are very pathetic, a big trench is dug and the boxes laid in a row. A little earth is thrown over when the first line is complete and then they start the second row above, a rough cross is made from a bully beef case with the name in pencil, and that is the end. These little crosses are found all over the country and many are buried where they fell. The health of the troops is very good but when the spring comes it will be very different with so many horses and men so hastily buried, and often half out of the earth. I see Uncle Willie is coming out, he does not know what he is coming to. The clergy have to work with the doctors and both mess together. The dressing stations where they work are simply appalling. I have seen and smelt them when the wounded came in on my wagons. They lay them in long rows in the field and you have to pick out the dead from the live in lamplight, a very difficult thing to do. There is a great row if you take a dead one as the space in the wagons is so limited. I hope you had a good Christmas. The men here had a very good time, and everything went on as usual. All the dogs here have to do something for their living. They drag carts about, or are put in a big wheel like a squirrel's cage and by walking work round the wheel and this turns a churn to make butter. A happy new year to you all whatever it may bring.

Coy – Company
****

****

Letter 7

ASC France

All well yet. The weather is very unsettled but we get some warm days now and again. I am glad the *zepps* did not come over be sure and see that you are not looking out of the windows when they come I hear that they have to keep all the blinds down just now to keep the war workers from looking out. The horses are all well and have stood the winter well I have had two died and six evacuated but this is not bad as they stand out in all weathers the health of the men is splendid and apart from accidents, kicks etc there is very little bother. We have done a lot of shifting since we came here, the villages are very picturesque and on the whole clean now the spring has come the country will be beautiful, all round us are hills rather like our own but not many trees and what there are are all down in the valleys by the river. The country is covered with troops and you never get away from war but sometimes we take a walk down by the river. I hope Mildred is well, it is so nice to be good, but the funny thing about this weary world is that everything that is either worth doing or having is wrong or indigestible. We have a good billet with an old Frenchman who was a prisoner in the last Franco German war. We had a drunk chained in his hen house the other night and his wife came to me in terror calling torrents of French. I found that some humorist had told her that he was some very dangerous German prisoner that was to be shot at dawn up against her house and she was terrified in case some damage had been done to her property.

Mildred – family friend of William Brown
Zepps – zeppelins
****

No 2 Company R.A.S.C, 7th Division. 1914 France

Letter 8

ASC France

All well yet. Things have brightened up a bit and the Germans have had a go at our village. It's really very annoying as you really never feel safe now. When I was shaving they slung in a shell. It fell in the street just outside my window. Every pane of glass in the street was shattered. Unfortunately, our horses were being led out to water and the result was bad. When I ran out two men were down, one instantly killed, the other kicked a bit before he died. One flew aimlessly up and down the street, shrieking and shouting, his shoulder was away and he died in hospital. Six big work horses lay all around. A good bag that for one shell! It was a quaint sight in this old world street, the dead looked so quiet in the grey morning light. Within ten minutes the place was itself again and nothing remained except the pools of blood. Then we finished shaving and had our breakfast. Unfortunately all the windows in the house were broken and now it is very cold, but they are being put right. After two months of quiet this is a pity for others may come and it destroys our piece of mind.

****

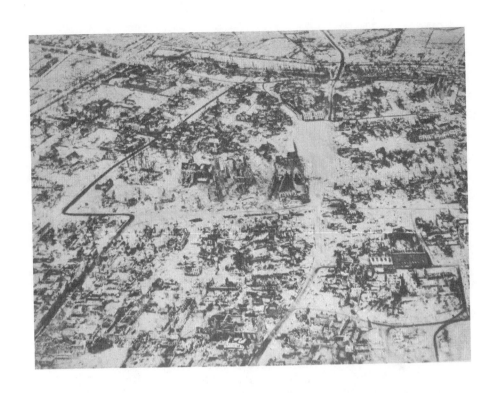

Ypres

****

Letter 9

ASC France

All well yet. Things very lively. The wagons have had some narrow escapes from shells. Five burst over them last night but neither man nor horse was hit. The Germans must have seen the camp fires as we were in a thick wood. The confusion was awful but we got hooked in somehow and made off down the road when two more shells burst over us but no damage was done. A tremendous battle is raging just now, and we take up the food after dark. It is a very nervous business as the place seems to be infested with spies who seem able to let the enemy know when the wagons are passing certain parts of the roads. The shells always seem to be too high. The wounded and refugees are pouring in and at night you see the burning villages all round. We have plenty of food but the weather is bad and the long rides in the rain are wearisome. We generally get in a house at night in a deserted village or farm. The refugees are awfully poor people, old and lame and sick, without homes, food or anything, tramping in the rain before the shells. Some of them who can't go fast enough get hit and that keeps up the pace of the others. The Germans are said to be losing a lot of men but we see very little of them and have only the shells to be afraid of.

****

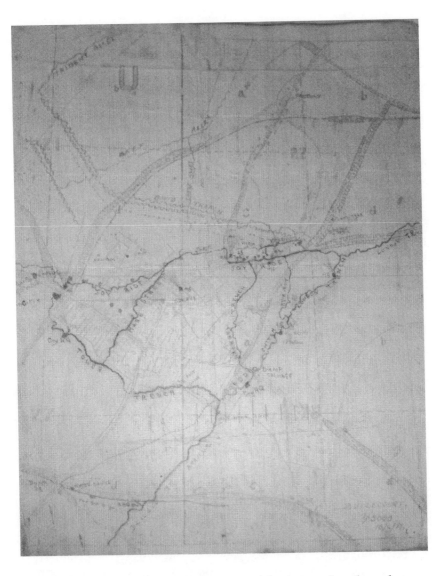

Copy of map of Bullecourt with Army landmarks

****

Letter 10

ASC France

All well yet. We are fairly in the thick of it and our division has suffered severely we had an attack of aeroplanes today and it was awful having to stand and wait for the bombs. One smashed a French hospital near and it was pitiful for us to see the poor wounded beggars tumbling out of their beds and dragging themselves out of the doors. The aeroplanes came slowly over us again and everyone waited and wondered who was to be killed. Then the bomb came right amongst us, and the whole scene was blotted out with dust and dirt thrown into the air. When it cleared away we found that five horses and two men had been killed. It gets on your nerves this business far worse than the shell fire, as in the dark you don't notice them coming. Things are very slow just now as both sides are fighting for the supremacy, and this will not be decided for some time. I have to gallop through villages that have been shelled by the Germans and its a real sporting event. A staff officer sent off a wagon every time there was a lull, and we galloped by the light of the burning houses. Not one wagon was hit but an unfortunate medical corps man got half his head off. We have some trying times at night bringing down the wounded. The wretched shattered men jog along in our springless wagons for miles in the rain. This is the time when we really come under rifle fire, but as it is in the early dark you do not notice it so much.

****

Letter 11

ASC France

All well yet. You would read about the last battle. I have had a bad cold but am better. The only room I can get now has had a shell right through and although water tight is very cold at night. We are in a smashed factory, both Germans and French had a go at it and there is nothing left but bare walls and twisted machinery. I wish you could see the town, whole sides are blown off houses and the furniture hangs over the edge of the floors. Many of the people are going about injured and I saw one old woman of about 70 with her whole head covered with bandages. Really, you cannot describe the effect in a house of the high explosive shell. I came through the town the other night by moonlight. It was as light as day and the empty smashed houses with the ruined church tower behind made a fine effect. On the church door is a large figure of Christ with the head knocked off. I got *Muffie's* letter about the women getting the jobs and I am glad I am here as no women are allowed. The territorial's must be very sick at not getting over its annoying the anti climax of repeated good byes. Poor old Gillig theatrical to the end. I didn't think he would carry his queer ideas out at such a time. I'm glad you got the films they are good and if you get them enlarged by a first class man should be a fine souvenir. Perhaps you should take them to Edinburgh. Give them the films, not the print, to the photographer and don't print from them until you get them back. Keep all the things carefully I send till I come back. Your parcels have come and are very nice. Life is more rosey just now as I managed to buy a barrel of beer which cheers us up a bit. The *Taube's* are very troublesome and give us some nasty

Letter 11 (continued)

frights occasionally. Two little children were killed near us, about 100 yards from our refilling point. You would notice it in the papers perhaps. You know how we get the food to the troops. First by train, then by motor lorry, then we take it up to the troops. Don't believe the rot in the papers about the motor lorries. They are never within five miles of a fight and very few have ever seen shell.
W

Gillig – family friend of William Brown
Muffie – friend or relative of William Brown
Taube's – Observational Planes

****

Letter 12

ASC France

I got the letters and parcels alright. Thanks very much. I appreciate them awfully. I sent from Lyndhurst a pair of leggings and boots. If you can send them on they would be very useful. The weather is not like June in Scotland but frosty at night. The greatest battle of the war is going on, our lots are fighting for their very existence, no one has gained an inch and we have at it for sixteen days, someone must give in in a day or two. Night and day the guns thunder, and when we take the transport up at night, the shells are awful. Away in the distance you hear a whisper which gradually becomes a whine, then a screech over you, and a crash. Whenever you hear the screech you are safe, as the shrapnel bursts forward but all the same it feels as if everyone was going to hit you on the chest. We had a big shell amongst us last night, two men and three horses killed and the rest of us scared out of our lives. Nerves are beginning to tell now and a sudden crash makes everyone jump. I enclose a bit which was driven in the wagon for an inch and a half. This is a nice thing to be floating about when you are having your peaceful sleep. The sunsets are magnificent here, and the whole country is shrouded in gold and purple, just like a mauve picture. There and here the burning villages throw a glow on the sky and the roar of the guns makes the scene most impressive. After dark thousands of troops march along the roads, broken by the lines of transport and long strings of ambulances. The shattered burned villages are pathetic sometimes with the late owner's half out of their doors where the shrapnel has got them. The refugees are everywhere and don't seem

****

Letter 12 (continued)

very much annoyed. The oldest people I have ever seen are
here, and get wheeled along in barrows, their burning
homes behind them. There is not much time to read, but
we like a paper. The 'Daily Mail' arrives in the camp
regularly and cheers us up with idiotic stories of victories.
We know here it is one of the toughest propositions that
have ever been tackled. Good luck whatever happens.
Mind and keep the plate full.
Willie

****

****

Letter 13

All well yet. You would see that I am in a new army now and in a new place. Our poor old division has been in it again and has done splendidly. We had some interesting times and our town was shelled but nothing serious. Now we are resting in the country but will be in it again at once. This part of France is lovely. Orchards and green fields of rows of poplars and many hedges. We are staying in a ruined chateau which must have been lovely once. There is a moat all round and hundreds of frogs make the night hideous. The nightingales sing also and this is a disappointing affair after Keats Ode and gets very tiresome. Probably he never tried to sleep through a din like this after a hard days work. Its sometimes very cold here but I am brown as a berry, I am awfully well and as thin as a lathe but this is splendid. Tell *Buggles* that the dog on the farm did six hours on the wheel yesterday, but he is a good dog and tried to please.

Buggles – family pet dog

****

Les Halles d'Ypres - Photo taken in 1912

Les Halles d'Ypres - Photo taken in 1914

****

Les Halles d'Ypres - Photo taken in 1916

****

Letters 14 - 32 were written in France when William Brown was a Lieutenant in the 2nd Battalion, Gordon Highlanders

****

Letter 14

2nd Gordon's France

All well yet but very miserable conditions. I would never have believed that human beings could be so uncomfortable. We live a queer life forty feet below the ground. Above is a very abomination of desolation. The mud is indescribable, knee deep. Candles are very much wanted here also we sat in six inches of water for a whole day in the dark and it was miserable, but we manage to keep cheery. I have seen some queer things lately as we are on new ground. I went up to the *BATTN*. Very easily and enjoyed. We hope to get out for Christmas. Some mufflers for the men would be alright. This is written in the dug out, bully and biscuit ahead. We took three dead Bosch out to make room so it is not so bad, safe at any rate. I got lost the other night, from 10am till 6pm a cheerful experience. I slept in a shell hole for some hours but it was raining so had to keep on the move and it was exciting as I did not know whether I was in our own or German lines. Write soon it is very dreary; there is no pomp and circumstance.

BATTN – Battalion

****

****

Letter 15

2nd Gordon's France

All well yet. Spring is showing signs of arriving, at least when it is not raining it is fairly hot in the sun. The villages are surrounded by apple trees, thousands of them and it will be a great sight when they are all in blossom. It is rather amusing to us to see the inhabitants coming back to the captured villages and having a look at what was once their home. In most cases not a vestige remains, poor souls they look rather glum. Isn't it strange to think of it? These people have lived for generations in their little homes, probably never been ten miles from them, and now they are scattered over France with nothing to come back to and very little to look forward to, for it will be years before the land can be used and a man with a plough would get some frights with 'dud' bombs and shells buried out of sight. I met a man from the base who was just out of hospital. He had slept in a hut some of the new women workers had put up and had nearly died of exposure. Poor fellow, he was glad to get up among the shells away from the woman's work. A very nice man who supported two aged uncles as well as a wife and four children. I am having a fairly quiet time just now as my men are all ready. I find the new men are very quick in the up take and not at all nervous and in dealing with bombs this is a great advantage. It will be strange to leave this life after the war. The living in dug out and learning to eat and sleep in crowded surroundings with constant noise will be hard to forget. The food is very monotonous now as we are not near any big towns and bully beef is our constant companion. The salmon will have a fine welcome when he comes. I am sending you

****

Letter 15 (continued)

today some newspapers that the Germans fling over for us. You might let me know when all these things arrive. I sent off a dagger this morning. Hope it will arrive alright.

****

****

Letter 16

2nd Gordon's France

It is astonishing how long this cold has lasted its colder than ever today and yet some of the trees are budding. You would be surprised to see a wood here after a 'doing'. The whole thing disappears, all colour disappears and only a succession of blackened stumps, with even the bark torn off them remains. All the leaves and branches are buried under tons of earth thrown up by 'heavies', and in a few days the whole extent of wood perhaps many acres is turned into an appalling grey coloured wilderness, which it is impossible to describe. The birds have gone off a few hawks knock about the trenches after rats, and do not seem to mind the shells. Very few crows come near the lines but there are thousands further back, grey backed with a beak that can open a plum and apple tin. One night in 'no mans land' we heard geese. It was strange to lye there on our backs and hear the inferior creations hurrying away from these wasted and vanished villages, while the superior creation feed up and rain their best to send there. For a long time we listened to the flocks honk honking across the sky no doubt wondering at the star shells beneath them that make night day. French rats are everywhere you see them in dozens and they certainly clean the place up, but they are very foul and run over your face at night. We very seldom bother to kill them so you would be surprised how tame they get. There are lots of wild cats also, they run away from the ruined towns and villages, and now make a precarious living round the trenches. A few dogs but not many as they usually get shot at sight, they have been know to carry information.

****

****

Letter 17

2nd Gordon's France 1916

All well yet. The weather has been frightful and we are exposed owing to German frightfulness. Heavy snow has made everything very miserable. All signs of spring have disappeared, but the year is getting on and it is bound to improve some time. Everywhere are signs of the Germans two and a half years tenure here. Every village has miles of wire round it and heaps of refuse, graves well kept and covered with wreaths to Fritz and Hans. Of course you have read about the villages and fruit trees. I sent you a little box of souvenirs the other day picked up in a captured village. I am also sending you a saw bayonet it is a nice thing to get in you. They invent some cheery weapons for our entertainment. I am afraid the war is not over by any means. It is going to be a different thing to go at the Germans now with this slow retirement. The machine gun has made a revolution in war fare and the rear guards are now most formidable. We must hope for the best and a quick finish and trust we will not have another winter. I am afraid leave is very far off, there is not so much now and this life gets rather tiresome, continually training or assaulting. The villages are all the same and the country is all the same. All is good in their own way but a change does us all good.

****

****

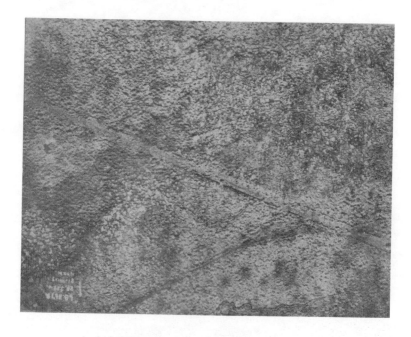

Ariel View of Menin Road, France

****

****

Letter 18

2nd Gordon's France

We are constantly on the move now and I am so bad with rheumatism that I can hardly write but my cold is now better. *Rae Brown* went through our village with his *battery* today but I did not see him. A pity for we are going different ways. The billets are very bad now and everything is very damp and wet, but I think even the mud is better than the frost. It has been an education to me all this seeing the French ways but I doubt if we would ever be able to make the people live such hard working lives. There are some good houses among the farms, but the majority are poor dirty places with stone floors and damp walls from which weary looking wall paper droops. Box beds of the old type, real consumption traps, are in the kitchen covered with filthy bed clothes. Dust, dirt, and rubbish are everywhere, every kind of old clothing and dirty utensils are treasured and stored under beds, in corners and everywhere where dust can gather. There is generally a square of tumbled down buildings in various states of decay. Wooden frames with a frame of plaster of clay, form these houses, and every kind of animal is housed in the most unlikely places. Hens, dejected ducks, a goose or two, a wretched donkey, bored goats, hundreds of rabbits getting ready for the food shortage, dogs of all kinds, pigeons, lean wild looking cats and some good horses, awful cows, skin and bone with awful sores on them, and rooting all over the place huge sows as thin as rakes, with huge families fighting over what the war has brought them. All the manure is placed in the middle of the yard and everything takes a turn at trying to get something

Letter 18 (continued)

to eat there and then retires to its den in the little dark houses. The houses are always thatched or tiled and never rainproof. The well is generally near the middle, and there is no sanitation of any kind what so ever. The people are kind in the main but very greedy and of course the war has soured them. They miss their sugar very much, it is too dear now but they appear to have plenty of food of one kind and another. They do not know much about the war and cannot understand how it has lasted so long. They work from morning to night and never read the papers, and wonder why the British are there at all.

battery – Battalion

****

****

Letter 19

Letter from Lt W N Brown received 30th Jan

Now you can rest easy for a few weeks for I will be in no danger. Its fine to get into a billet and have some warmth and comfort. All your parcels have come and have been very much appreciated by the men and if ever you see anyone who sent anything to me explain to them what happened to me. I must get onto my correspondence next week. We have had exciting times since I came back but I am not hurt. I have grand luck, but I lost two of my best bombers, both special favourites but they were buried where they fell in the ghastly wilderness. It is impossible to describe the 'no mans land'. I have never read any proper description of it, it's the greyness of it, the actual want of colour, the endless succession of holes and mounds, shattered timbers sticking up from mud, endless abandoned trenches, rows of trees halved, or stripped into poles, the extraordinary amount of abandoned equipment bombs, rifles, clothing, and the dead amongst it all, quiet, not repulsive, fitting into the drab scene, sometimes German sometimes English. In twos or threes as they were killed, or one by himself, lonely even in this lonely place. The pools of water in the shell holes are green or red, and over the endless stumps and twisted broken wires rises the sour smell of battlefield. I got a Christmas card from Charlie which I send back to you as a souvenir with the rev MacLean Watts little contribution. The old Fritz who wrote the field postcard to his friend at the front will never see him again. You must thank Annie very much for her present it is very kind of her to remember me, and I

****

Letter 19 (continued)

appreciate it very much. They say out here that Lord French was very pleased with the volunteers and immediately after inspecting them started a campaign in favour of total prohibition. Of course all the red noses may have been with the cold, but the general said that it was impossible that they could have been got with eating oranges, and that something would need to be done and that quickly. I saw today about a woman that got a month for smoking a cigarette in a munitions factory. This just shows what is going on. I hope poor Hughes feet are better. He will have to sign the pledge an awful thing to do. I hope Connie is not getting any more disappointments with her soldiers wives. I hear that they got an awful fright when the Kaiser proposed peace as they thought that they would need to stop all their picture houses and whisky if peace came. Their does not seem to be much chance of peace yet Germany is a wonderful nation they have put Romania right and that leaves them free to attend to other places for they seem to have plenty of men. Now I must draw to a close. Good luck to you all. Willie

****

"No Man's Land"

It is impossible to describe the "No Man's Land." I have never read any proper description of it. It's the greyness of it, the actual want of colour, the endless succession of holes & mounds, shattered timbers sticking up from the mud, endless abandoned trenches, rows of trees halved or stripped into poles, the extraordinary amount of abandoned equipment, bombs, rifles, clothing, and the dead amongst it all, quiet, not repulsive, fitting into the whole scene, sometimes German sometimes English, in twos or threes as they were killed, or one by himself, lonely even in this lonely place. The pools of water in the shell holes are green or red, and over the endless stumps and twisted broken wires rises the sour smell of the battlefield —

Copy of an original letter

****

****

Letter 20

Jan 1917

I am not up with the line yet, but half way, and quite well again it will not be long now until I am with the battalion again, but you do not need to worry as we will be quite safe for some time. It has been awful weather, snow and rain, but it has to be put up with until it dries up and then the war may be over. I haven't had any letters from you for some time, but will get a bunch when I get back. All my parcels, too, have gone down deserving throats, as it is mess rule to open them if the unfortunate owner is away. They were very good to me in hospital, but it is tiresome, but the *V.A.D.'s* are fine but it takes the ward sister looking after them. The men do all the real hard work. But we had a good time at Christmas. Wuffie would enjoy it as there is always smashing of plates or something, or people swallowing thermometers. One man had a temperature of a 103 and the VAD only put down 100 on his chart so as not to make the doctor nervous. That is what goes on. One man got appendicitis in the hospital and they found three thermometers in his appendix. It was very sad, a nice man who supported an aged aunt and had a wife and four small children. They had deducted the price of the thermometers from his pay but I heard that there was a movement on foot to have the matter put before the authorities at home with a view to having the money refunded.

V.A.D – Voluntary Aid Detachment

****

Ariel photo of the aftermath, France

****

Letter 21

March 14th 1917

Not much time to write just now. It's very cold again and the mud is bad. I've got over the rheumatism but I feel the cold. I am sending you a few more odds and ends, not much use, but they give you some idea. These things are from the nearest dug out to Germany. The general desolation is difficult to describe, but the grass is coming up and there is a faint green tinge over the miles of shell holes. It will be a blessing when it is high enough to cover up mans humanity to man. I came across a *BOSCH* the other day, the only one left above ground, on the top of a rolling hill, covered with the debris of war and torn with shells. The rain and the mud, the crows in the bitter wind, the smashed dug outs, and in the middle this lonely grave a fine contrast to the pomp and circumstance of war. Death has no dignity here, mud puts an end to all that. I enclose you a five marc note, it's rather rare to find any money on the Germans, and by looking at their pay books they seem to draw very little. We have got very good dug outs but off course the atmosphere in the places gets very bad, and if you did not get a walk out every now and again you would nearly choke. We cook tea on the *Tommy's* cookers and with bully beef and biscuits we do not do so badly. Of course you get some frights but that is to be expected and it is luck you want. Its alright thinking the readiness is all but that doesn't prevent one jumping head long into a shell hole when the five point nine comes along. The inhabitants of these parts will get a shock when they come back and find not a vestige of their village, let alone their houses left. Here and there you can see a miserable little patch

****

Letter 21 (continued)

with a broken gate all that is left of a garden, a few dead cabbages and here and there are rows or two, gone to briar. There is not a brick left of the house, a hole where the cellar was, and a jumble of broken indistinguishable rubbish, dreary flapping rags, and in one case a wooden horse, paintless, without a leg. There are tins everywhere, jam, bully beef and biscuit tins millions and millions littered in every corner. Tins show the progress of an army here. Apple trees are abound, every little house has its orchard, many of them smashed and twisted but tough to the last. This must have been a lovely district once, but now a desert would be fair in comparison. I doubt there will be no leave until 'the day'.

BOSCH / Tommy – German's

****

****

Letter 22

Letter from Lt W N Brown received 5th April 1917

All wet yet and flourishing. The country is absolutely ruined. Every house has been blown up with dynamite or *gun-cotton*, every little place absolutely ruined and the trees are all down. Millions of pounds of damage must have been done by the Germans in their retreat for they have hardly left one stone standing on another. Even the little orchards are finished every tree being cut down. The country is open and long rolling hills are the feature, with no hedges or ditches, hardly broken by a tree now the Germans are driven back, and every here and there a smashed aeroplane with its crew buried beside it, some of them years old. The last parcel was very much appreciated, and it is only with luck that you will get this letter. I suppose you have been reading in the papers about the German retreat. You wouldn't believe the damage they have done. Such petty kinds of thing, every apple tree little and big, poisoned all the wells with arsenic, spread filth about the roads and fields, destroyed the houses absolutely without remorse from the fine chateaux to the humblest little barn. There is not a house, however small, left and as the weather is very bad we have had rather a rough time. Not a stick of furniture is left; everything that could not be carried away has been piled up and burned. All over are mines with wires placed across paths, insulating placards put up on the shattered walls, in fact its difficult to follow the German mind at present. I think it will take France some time to recover after the war for even if we drive them out, they will turn the finest provinces of France into a desert. They are very strong and determined yet, and

Letter 22 (continued)

have plenty food, though few luxuries, and plenty good shells. The shells are far worse than the bullets, especially the big ones. I lay on a hill side the other day and watched them shell a place. You can hear the shell coming and then 'crump' a great cloud of black smoke and you see everyone rushing out and making for the open like bees out of a hive. Five went in and there were no casualties though the explosions were terrific. The black smoke is often as red as blood with the powdered bricks. The weather is awfully bad and we have no blankets, nothing but what we can carry, so you hardly get any sleep with the cold. Bitter winds sweep over the hills and showers of snow and hail go on day and night. I have lost one or two good friends the last few days. You would be pleased to see the snowdrops here coming up among the shattered bricks everywhere around. The Germans have put them on all their graves and before they left decorated the crosses with wreaths. I found a young German lying where he had fallen on the great rolling grass slopes. A boy of about 20, Fritz Witte, and buried him. He must have been one of the last to leave after blowing up the houses. I got the salmon alright and Wuffies parcel alright and it was splendid as we can buy nothing now and we had a fine dinner in a patched ruin. There's plenty wood and with big fires you are fairly comfortable. If you send me out a couple of pipes I would like. Big bowls are best and straight stems, not expensive ones. Let me know if you ever got the little dagger. It was rather neat. W N Brown

gun-cotton – explosive propellant

Letter 23

April 21st 1917

All well yet. The weather is improving but still windy. We are in a wood at present all the place is covered with the wastage of war and a good thing too in this cold weather for it makes good fires. In the parcel I sent you there is a Bosch pipe I picked up and two of the cases of German bombs that we use as shaving mugs. The little bottle came from a place where there was the savagest fighting in the line. Magpies and hawks are the only birds seen here and a few partridges but the Bosch seems to have killed off all the game birds. Strangely enough when marching through one shattered wood, so bad that hardly a tree stood up, an owl was knocking about trying to locate his late peaceful home. Every living thing that is wise clears off when Fritz is around. The French must be pretty sick with affairs just now, even though we are pushing the Bosch out, he is leaving a desert behind him, and it will take years to rebuild the countryside. The sinking of new wells to replace the poisoned and contaminated ones will be a big job for this is at best a waterless country. Poisoned food is left about and hundreds of brutal traps with high explosives to maim and kill. It may be war but science has put it in human being ways to be cruel. A lot of the country has been cultivated but a lot is lying idle and must be getting in a very bad state, and every 'sucerie' has been destroyed. These 'suceries' are enormous buildings with the latest and finest machinery and their loss will be serious as they will take along time to replace. I lived in a 'sucerie' and was very comfortable until one day the inevitable came. We all rushed out like rabbits when a

Letter 23 (continued)

ferret is at his job, and from the hill watched our little home getting straffed. There is hardly ever a casualty so it is rather interesting when you are far away and the walls and roofs are flying to the skies. It is always a worry wondering if your kit has gone. There were eight men sleeping in an enormous boiler and a nine inch shell fell at its side and rolled it over two or three times and I tell you the men had a festive time but no one was hurt and it made it very amusing. These places are shell traps but the comfort is worth the risk. The first cow slip is out now and near the door of our billet, a noble effort as we had snow two days ago. A parcel has just arrived and is splendid. We have no fresh potatoes now and I miss them very much, but a parcel makes a fine change. We are really very well fed. Two of my friends have died in hospital but thank goodness we have done so well that the casualties were not serious. I have to start and train more men when we come out for a lot of good men go under. We will need a lot of men for Fritz is not finished yet by any means, and apart from dirty tricks he is a great fighter.

sucerie – factory / sugar shack

****

****

Letter 24

April 27th 1917

The parcels have come, also the shirts. Really I have never needed them so badly. The Germans must have been very dirty. We are 'in' just now but it is tolerably quiet. *'Business Risks'* and that is not so bad. I don't think the Bosch likes to have our people about, he never straffs us like he does some of the other divisions. It's remarkable to see the little towns that have grown up every where in the great rolling downs since we first went over them. There was not a soul to be seen then and now the place is covered with every kind of little shelter behind which men can creep out of the bitter winds. These little shelters are most ingenious and though not rain proof give their makers a place to lie in. Many of them are just holes dug in the banks and sunk roads, and it is remarkable how healthy the men keep in this new life. The men who have been out a while at once look round and see how to make themselves comfortable, and all kinds of stoves, chairs and even looking glasses appear in the dug outs, while plates pots and pans overlooked by the Bosch, make things a bit more comfortable. It's astonishing the thorough way the place has been cleared, however. All that is left is hardly worth picking up. The dug out is not much good. We are passed all the German ones now and the ones you come across and look very inviting, you dare not go into in case of traps. Some of the traps are most ingenious and show the Bosch to be in possession of a perverted sense of humour. Souvenirs are left about, helmets etc. Which when touched fire the mines. He's a painstaking sole and overlooks nothing.

'Business risk's - Bullets and small shells not big shells

****

Letter 25

Letter from Lt W N Brown 2 . 5 . 17
All well yet in spite of cold winds and Germans. I'm glad that you got the box of souvenirs and hope the bayonet comes let me know when it does. The flag I found beside an aeroplane, a French one, which had crashed down in the German lines long before we advanced, and which lay a crumpled mass of wreckage beside the hasty grave of the two airmen. The two bombs sent you are quiet safe I emptied them and sent them over with a friend as they are not allowed to go through the post. They are German. I have sent you also a watch I got in a sunken road after we had taken it. The parcels are coming all right and are much appreciated, but don't run into too much expense, we get good rations. Don't send them every week; every fortnight will do quite well. I saw a man today. He brought up a small draft, I forget his name, but he used to play hockey at Melrose. He was a master at *St Mary's*. We come on a good many fields here that have been cultivated recently and it is refreshing to see them. It will be a pity if the Hindenburg line has to be reduced to a desert before we get through. Of course, the weeds and rank grasses are covering up the Somme front. In a few months this waste of mud will be gone as an example of a modern battlefield. Mores the pity. The site of it might have made some future disturber pause, though it's doubtful if it would have stopped him. What fun for the women when they vote declaring they are over 35. Very few will go at all its all the old ones that like a drop of whisky in their tea so that makes the drink all right. No fear now that's it being stopped.
St Mary's – School in Melrose, Scottish Borders

****

Letter 26

May 16th 1917

All well yet. Have just come out and had another splendid success. This is the second successful assault within a month. I never went through anything like it. We were under shell fire, 5.9s, for two days and only a six foot bank to lie under, I have just got orders to go up again, cheerful!!!! Well, I'm back again – the worst time I have ever had. However I am out all well so it is not so bad. The Germans are putting up a terrible fight. I'm glad you got the watch alright, isn't the saw bayonet a beauty, nice to get it to you. They are a strange nation producing the reformation and poisonous gas, the most beautiful hymns and the saw bayonet. I hope it will end soon. We have had enough. MacLean Watts article was very good. I remember the night well, but it can hardly be described, imagine being stuck in the mud to the waist and shrapnel being played on you. The only thing is that the misery is so awful that you hardly mind. However, it has got to be gone through. I was coming back to headquarters that night and dived down a shell hole was quiet lucky. The grass and trees are showing life now and the larks sing even up near the front line, while all over the downs you see the last years crop making an attempt to come up. Everywhere the grass is covering up the broken houses and ruined trenches and the more terrible result of mans inhumanity are at least getting a veil. You can look out when it is quiet and the scene is as peaceful as if it was at home, and in a few minutes it is a raging hell of black smoke, dust and indistinguishable things. The trees lie in every direction and this makes the landscape dull and uninteresting. The

****

Letter 26 (continued)

houses are gradually disappearing, the bricks on the roads, the ribs for firewood so the villages are passing, kultur has done its work.

****

****

Letter 27

Rced. 26 / 5 / 1917

All well yet and having a good time, but its work from morning till night. Our last assault was a terror but we gained all our objectives. We moved in after dark and crept into line on a long dark hill slope, only lit up occasionally by the shell bursts, and waited for the dawn. It's a cheerful affair the waiting, you are bound to be discovered sometime, and the Bosch lets loose a shower of 5.9s on selected spots on speck at intervals. You have plenty of time for meditation which takes queer forms. Then the first streaks of dawn, one of our guns goes off, and then absolute pandemonium. Swish, swish, go our shells over your head in endless streams and old Fritz opens up. The noise and smells are bad and some of the sights are bad but it is astonishing how few are hit. Then you look at your watch for the 365th time and over you go. The machine guns crack, when they crack the bullets pass you but you forget that. A wall of bursting shells move in front of you and into the mass of ruins, once a village, you go. Then you see the first Bosch running out, hands up, 'Kamerading', till a bayonet stops him, and then twos and threes, and then scores rushing through the smoke, the Lewis guns having the time of their lives, and crying, their voices lost in the din of the shells and the savage yells of our men half mad with blood over the ruins of house and orchard, a machine gun, manned to the last, holds up the line, the bombers swing round it, rifle grenades add to the din and it stops. On again, the rifle men over their dead and wounded and then what's left of the gun crew are 'for it'. Then the objective, furious digging, rushing up and down, stores up, guns in position, and then comparative quiet. Both side draw off to lick their sores, but not for long. The wounded are got off, dug outs explored, terrified Bosch got out by peaceful persuasion or a bomb, and the position is taken. When the smoke clears away, the bright sunlight reveals every sordid detail of a mechanical war. Stores lie in every direction, everything broken, and every here and there a man, twisted into dreadful attitudes, but with quiet faces they lie where they fell, the dust veiling the wounds, finished with it all. The Bosch is certainly not starving. I had cold coffee a fresh egg and plenty good bread in the dug out, and there were tins of meat, brandy, rum, sardines (English). An officer was at the foot of the stairs, nobody heeding him, splendidly made, with a good face. The deep dug out is fine after the din above. The fumes make you sick and drowsy, but the work is only starting. All the pockets of the dead Germans are gone through and the papers sent to headquarters. There are some sad photos, wives and children, little groups taken in happy times: letters from their people, diaries with fervent hopes for peace: picture postcards in thousands, one showing the French marching out of Verdun as prisoners rather premature.

W N B

****

****

Letter 28

July 16th 1917

All well yet. We are living in some discomfort in very deep dug outs, and they are needed. When things are quiet you can wander round what was once the villages, now a mass of skeleton roofs and heaps of bricks. The gardens have made a great effort but the constant shelling gives nothing a chance so you come on all the old fashioned flowers, half in shell holes and forcing their way through bricks and tiles. Sweet Williams, roses of all kinds, lupins, and pansies make a fine show in the sheltered corners. We get some cabbages here and there, and one lucky man found a bed of asparagus. The ruins of the village are pathetic. You can't help visualizing the time when those broken stoves, chairs, bedsteads, crockery, torn clothing, and odds and ends, were someone's treasures. All the little gardens have been well kept at one time, but they are gone now for the owner's lifetime at least. In one of those little corners you come on, even in the worst places, which seem to escape the hail of shells, a mass of ramblers over a summer house. The grass round is rank and is choking the flowers, but it is a delight to see it in such a desert. At the door was a human foot whether English or Bosch I cannot tell. The swallows stick to their villages in spite of it all, and build in the ruins, and so hard up are they for suitable sites that they invade our shelters and get so tame that they carry on during the worst straif. The sparrows and rats flourish as usual, but the sparrows have a disreputable look. Their life is a misery keeping out of the way of stray cats that slink about, wild and hungry, all their well fed contempt for their owners gone, fear now in their eyes, the

****

Letter 28 (continued)

flies are bad now, great green fellows, clustering in
thousands in certain parts of the parapet, and you know
what is beneath. However, taking things all round it is not
too bad, for the line, and as the weather is good you can
enjoy life a bit. If it would only look like finishing it would
be easier to bear. It is a pity we have another winter to face
but I suppose it has to be. I saw 200 little girls marching in
Boulogne with a substantial major at the head, all in khaki,
and very self conscious.

****

****

Letter 29

France October 1917

Arrived back, had a dreadful crossing. Really the sea is awful to people who are not used to it. We are resting now but the weather is very bad, and rain as usual. The country here is very flat, but there are long ridges well wooded, and here and there quiet sharp little hills, big mounds in fact with little villages on the top, and the inevitable windmills. When the sun sets the effect is very wonderful as the woods are more irregular than is usual here, and so look more like our own. The long lines of poplars never please me though they have an atmosphere of their own in the canal countries. Really you can hardly imagine how war alters a countryside. For anyone newly out the traffic is most interesting. The confusion seems hopeless, though to the older eyes it is perfectly ordered. Strings of wagons, carts, troops, guns, stores, every kind of horse, mule, pony, etc. Move slowly along. All the fields are full of depots or horse lines, every house has men hanging about the doors, cleaning their rifles, smoking and waiting, and this goes on night and day all to keep the mud smothered men in the front line and the guns pounding away. It is very cold now and I could do with a Shetland jacket. Mind this that if anything comes my way either good or bad there must be nothing in the papers except the mere notice, don't forget.

****

****

Letter 30

October 5th 1917

All well yet. We have just come out of the worst action I have ever seen. I got through again, my luck is great. Many good chaps have gone out, some of my old friends, Callum Graham got his arm taken off and died. The mud is awful, it makes life impossible and yet we go on. We are back in a nice quiet place, not even bombs at night, and maybe for sometime but you never can tell. Those Italians are the limit. The German strength is wonderful; I am beginning to think that there are only three fighting nations. Winter is coming on us and there is not much hope of comfort for some time to come, however, we have got the thanks of parliament and that is always something. If you could send me a kippered salmon it would be much appreciated and a change. It's a strange thing to see the war zone, once a lovely wooded country covered with little farms, the red roofs just showing through the trees, and now a desert is the most dreadful aspect, not a tree remaining, shattered stumps show where they once stood. You can stand on the high ridges and gaze over to the German territory in the distance, where the war has not yet carried and visualize the desolation yet to come. Chateaux and farms have gone in the zone. Roads are obliterated, streams are now immense marsh and mud, this is only the broad view, the details of war scattered broadcast over all are really too horrible, but the mud hides all and nature has covered these parts with a gay blanket of weeds. Nothing good will grow where war has passed, but still in this waste the guns roar and shells churn the ground

****

Letter 30 (continued)

unendingly, death is nothing, life is nothing, carrying out of orders is all. However behind the lines things go on in the same old way, old people live out their lives, a little extra toil for all, men grow up in the villages, news of death and wounds come to little houses, occasionally aeroplanes smash the life out of a few wretched peasants, and the war goes on.

****

****

Letter 31

Letter from Lt W N Brown November 29th 1917

Just time for a few lines. I have been ill unfortunately, a bad dose of fever, got well then a relapse, but I think I am clear of it now though not well yet. I got a nice letter from Aunt May, it was nice to hear about home, would we were all back. Also your letter which was most welcome. I will write to you as often as I can but do not be anxious if the letters stop for a while for I am going on a long journey. So don't worry I won't be in action for a good while. That last action was enough to put you past war forever. Its fairly into Flanders winter. That is it rains every other day instead of every day in summer. The trees are all bare but the branches on the hedges still hold thin yellow red leaves and cover the country with a very Autumn atmosphere, depressing in the rain but almost beautiful when the sun breaks through. The fields are lonely without the bird life to which we are accustomed. Even the sheep and the *whaups* in our own hills keep the silence from becoming too profound. A few magpies poke round the rubbish heaps and towards dark and old hoodie swings noiselessly over from some dreadful spot in the line. No cheery rooks making for their woods, even the sparrows are quiet, the Hawks swing far overhead, nothing but fighting men and birds seem to be happy here and with both, life and the small happiness that war allows depend on silence. This Italian business is awful. They were alright fighting Austrians quiet good in fact and inclined to 'stretch their necks' as soldiers say, over their little successes but the German is another proposition. It takes British or French

Letter 31 (continued)

troops to stand up to them. Its hard luck to have to go and fight for them now that we were beginning to think that we knew every shell hole on the British front. However, *C'est la Guerre.* Well it is a change anyhow whether it makes for war or peace. I doubt it is lengthening the war but you never can tell. I was awfully nearly into the hands of the women last week. Just touch and go, temperature 103 for two days, but I made a terrible effort and escaped. They didn't get me this time but it was a near thing. I shudder when I think of it. Poor things there are a lot of them getting killed now with the bombs, no peace anywhere. I met young Tom Ogilvie the other night, he was here to dinner and we had a great night, though I was far from well, he is a colonel on the railway transport now and is a great Gordon. He mentioned how well Gala had done in the war. How few have had to be conscripted. What a difference to die a volunteer, to those who live through even if maimed, what a pride to feel they went, were not compelled to go. I had a very sad duty lately, about the best friend I have made in this war, a young boy Dobbie a second Lt was killed by a Bosch sniper while binding up the wounds of another officer. He was fearless and has since got the MC. Before he went into action he asked me to write to a girl if he got it and curiously enough though he was from Glasgow the girl lived in Selkirk. She is a Miss Mary Linton in high street. I wrote to her but it was a sad job, I liked the boy so much. He and I did all our jobs together, good and bad. It's a queer lottery when he goes and I with ten more years of life am spared. I wonder

****

Letter 31 (continued)

if Joe Browns daughter would know Miss Linton. We could not get his body but he lies with a lot of stout men, where they fell. The Menin road will never be forgotten and it is close beside this ever lasting monument that he lies. Renwick of Hawick was badly injured, I saw him in the distance when he was going down. But it was no place to linger. He had a thumb off and his arm broken I think. Mein was not badly hurt and we have lost track of him. I hope you get news of him soon but once they are passed the *C.C.S* we get no news. Now this is not a very cheery letter but I still have a bit of fever and will write a better one next time.

Whaups – curlew
C'est la Guerre – It is War
C.C.S – Casualty Clearing Stations

****

****

Letter 32

December 11th 1917

There is nothing to do in those underground regions but write. It's safe however and one can feel the thuds overhead with pleasure. You could never imagine the life and I cannot describe it. The bombers have some awful fighting in those dug outs, real hand to hand, the prehistoric club and the grenade. It's a job to go down into the dark and clear out the Bosch. However, his loss is our gain and we find his blankets and cooking stoves very useful. Our old dug out was good but the present one is better. I had very bad luck yesterday; my orderly was sniped, poor sole, a very nice lad. He was walking behind me and I had a fine sprint over the open after he died, but I am alright and we are out now. We may be out at Christmas and if so will have a fine time so you might send me a box of kippers it will come in time to brighten up the feast. Where we are now it is all bully and biscuits, not bad but monotonous. I will send you some souvenirs soon, some tassels from the German Sergeants bayonet which show the regiment to which they belong, a German bombers club and a bayonet from a Sergeant dealt with in a forty foot dug out. I hope you are well and cheery. The war can't go on forever. I got the parcel and we had the salmon in the trenches on a brazier and I hope soon to have a night in the pyjamas.

****

Letters 33 – 47 were written in Italy when William Brown was in the 2nd Battalion, Gordon Highlanders

****

Letter 33

14 / 12 / 17

All well yet. You will have to address my letters now *B.E.F.* Italy. It's a great change, new scenes, new people and unhappily a new and dreadful language. Oh, the tower of Babel. What a curse to put on an enthusiastic if misguided public. The Alps are fine, great black snow flaked peaks imposing to the lowland people, but savage and bare to be avoided. The grandest scenery is in the vine country where rows of vines run up the mountain sides until one wonders how they are tilled and how the soil lies on these almost perpendicular slopes. The plains are endless and flatter than Flanders. Vines flourish everywhere. Curiously enough the local trees are all planted in rows and topped and then made to earn their keep by supporting families of vines which stretch from one to another for mile after mile. This system of live posts is about the best thing I have seen as yet. All the work is done by huge oxen, ploughing is very deep with always six and sometimes eight oxen. Progging and whacking them with sticks is about the hardest exercise Antonio uses. The houses are better built, not good in our sense of the word, but an improvement on the wood and mud structures in Flanders. Chickens, turkeys and ducks are in great abundance, in fact it looks as if it was never very cold here for there are newly hatched chickens running about and the half dead leaves are still on the trees. It is the difference of temperature between night and day that

****

Letter 33 (continued)

comes hardest on us. The cold at night is something awful, but it is warm in the daytime. The churches have all their steeples separate. White and red, and painted with fruit etc. Sometimes rather fine, but these things need blue skies. The kippers came alright. Please send some more, once a month or so if possible. We enjoyed them more than anything. Mind and address my letters now Italy instead of France. Another dozen razor blades are needed. That's about all.

W

B.E.F – British Expeditionary Force

****

****

Letter 34

Italy December 1917

All well yet and getting near Christmas. It is rather a dreary outlook. Everyone in the World I should think will be wondering if this is to be the last one. I have been in the mountains and there is not a great deal of snow, and on the lower planes the sun is quiet hot. The whole of the low country is lined with vines. It must be a great sight in autumn but the average wine is very thin and poor so I doubt if the grapes can be up to much. The houses are well built but are very cold as they are mostly constructed for heat. Stone floors and doors everywhere make life rather chilly at night. As it is hard frost then. There are no fires and the most primitive cooking arrangements, and of course the most primitive laws of sanitation are unknown. The rooms are rarely papered but are covered with painted flowers and fruits, crude in the extreme, the same artists no doubt that decorated our ice cream barrows at home. Roads are very good, very well kept, and lined with acacia, whose thorns make a fine barrier. It is very poisonous however and dangerous to animals. The whole effect is even flatter than Flanders, for the poplars there rather broke the monotony. Of course the great circle of the Alps is magnificent and holds the eye. Jugged, black and white with impossible houses tucked away into corners in impossible places. How they get up and down is a mystery; how they can live without fuel beats me, but live they do. The women as is usual in those agricultural countries are far finer than the men; they do most of the work, the men affecting the lighter accomplishments such as ice cream

****

Letter 34 (continued)

vending, street corner arguments etc. The thing to keep the women right is plenty of hard work. The children swarm everywhere, some perfect little beauties with every shade of olive, some almost black. Healthy, in fact much better looking in this respect than the French children who were always thin and underfed looking. They are little devils however and a terror to have about, nothing is safe, especially the food though they pinch the most useless things. We are getting English rations again, the Italian ones were rather awful and I never was a hand at macaroni. Beef too is rather poor as cattle have to do some useful work in ploughs and carts before easing the shortage of food. Unfortunate cows do their bit in the dairy line and then lug the proceeds to market; they are war workers if you like. The dogs however get a good time, no wheels here and every kind of dog you could imagine. I doubt we will get very few parcels for Christmas as we get very few mails here, but we hope for the best. I get very little time for writing letters as I am now *adjutant* and have a lot of work. I will send postcards when I can. There is one thing here the houses are well built and stand the shells and there is no bombing this gives you a rest. Good luck to you all and a good new year. Willie.

Adjutant – an officer who acts as administrative assistant to a superior officer

****

****

Letter 35

Italy 29th January 1918

All well yet but very busy. There is a good deal of snow now and that and the rain make things rather sticky. The rivers here run very fast and are deathly cold. They are either raging torrents or tiny streams. I expect when the snows melt that they will flood the plains. There are deep ditches everywhere to take the water off. The place is covered with mulberry trees to feed the silk worms festooned with vines. Some days the alps are as clear as water and you can see every little house. Again they are covered with great sweeping clouds. Or shrouded in light blue mists, with only the white crests in view. We are doing better for rations now, very well in fact. It's a great organisation that can bring the supplies of all kinds to all fronts in every climate. Everyone is cheery here and it is streets better than *'the salient'*. There are plenty of bombs but on the whole life is very uneventful. I sent a pair of field boots home some time ago and when you are next in London take them to Manfield's to be blackened. As I don't wear a kilt now I can wear them when I am riding. I never get a paper out here now but I understand all the women are to be sent back. Too many tied up thumbs and rather too many thermometers disappearing. Economy is all the thing now so men are stepping in. Good bye for the present and good luck. Willie

the salient – area around Ypres

****

Postcard marking training area used for
upcoming Piave assault

Letter 36

Italy February 1918

All well yet. It is a little while since I wrote to you, but we have been 'IN' and there is little time to spare. The country here is magnificent, the contrasts making most wonderful effects. The Alps tower into the skies, cold white against the blue, but down below the hills are warm brown and the vines and brushwood without their leaves give a neutral tint to the whole country. Nearly all the houses are white and stand out with a startling distinctness, many roofless, mere shells. The river flows swiftly, a cold clear stream over great beds of shingle, which it has carved by the spring floods into many channels all deep and dangerous. It looks like a place for trout but I doubt if the Bosch will encourage the milder form of Kultur, fishing, even granted that it is doing some unfortunate creature out if its life. I think that the ruin of some of these villages is a more pitiable sight than the French ones. Here few of them are smashed but 'wars awesome blast' has smashed everything to chaos and endless confusion, ones once prized possessions chucked into the street. Beds, splendid furniture, clothes, china, pictures, in one great sordid ruin. But it provides endless amusement to the troops, turning it over, coming on some useful article, decorating his funk hole with pictures mostly of dreary looking saints or papal dignitaries. Firewood is here in plenty, dry, and this is a matter of life and death here where keen eyed observers watch day and night for the little column of smoke that brings the quick shell. You can hardly believe what a picture it makes in the moonlight. The river bed pure white

Letter 36 (continued)

with the black stream, the low hills grey with the gleaming houses, and the peaks beyond rising out of the darkness. We have got good dug outs, rather comfortable but it is rotten down in the earth. I only wish that it were finished but I am afraid that this Russian thing has upset things. I am next for leave but am afraid it will be a long time as I am going on another long journey so don't worry if you do not get any letters for a long time. I hope Nell is holding her own it is a long war for her and she is too old for war work. I am sorry to hear about Wuffie, it is the same every year and comes from talking to everyone on the way up from the town on wet days. Half the *WAAC*'s get off duty with standing in the wet to talk to one another there are all men in the canteens now and that is a good job. I got your parcels alright. The salmon was eaten in the front line as far up as you could go so that fish has done its bit. I hope to be home soon but don't count on it. Good luck Willie

WAAC – Women's Army Auxiliary Corps

****

Letter 37

Italy June 1st 1918

All well yet and enjoying the sunshine. It's never too hot on the high hills. Really it is a wonderful place this plateau. Huge rocks, driven into white fragments cover the hills, while overall are the pines, growing in endless profusion and covering the whole land. There's a queer solemnity about these woods, the trees are so straight and they grow from every corner of the rocks. There is very little wind and the rumble of the guns echo down the valleys till lost in the gullies. Fallen trees are everywhere, knocked down by shells and broken by the snow and now and again in the tangle of under wood you come on the graves of friend or foe, thrown in where they fell, away back in 1916. There are no game birds or animal life among those rocks. I cannot describe the view from the top of the hills over the Lombardy Plaines. They stretch to Venice and the sea on one side, and into a soft mauve haze on the other, chequered with vines, tiny villages and pure white houses relieving the endless shades of green. The rivers run great bands of white shingle, with a thread of blue water into the distance the banks clustered with little groups of white, red roofed houses. Vines and acacia, lazy life in all forms, bullocks instead of horses, splendid women, swarming children of all tints from white to black, wine, cool recesses beneath endless arches, glorious fruit splashing the white streets with gold and crimson. Italy can never be enjoyed by northern nations. The flies and smells, the cruelty to animals and the heat, and the comfortless houses in the wintertime cannot balance the beauty of the hills. We find it difficult to breathe but get used to it and I

****

Letter 37 (continued)

am in splendid training now with climbing mule tracks.
We had a very nasty little scrap the other night. One of my
few old friends got it in the head. The other boy who went
out to bring him in was shot in the body and has since
died. Except for these little scraps which are always very
fierce there is little doing. There is nothing else to write
about and I am very well off. Of course there are no
WAASC's here and that is something to be glad about.

****

Letter 38

Italy June 21st 1918

All well yet. The heat has given way and torrents of rain
are falling. Every little stream bed is a torrent, and the river
reminds one of the *Ettrick* in spate. It runs faster but the
red water covers up the white shingle and with the help of
the bridges which are very like those at home, the effect is
very like. The vines are a great boon giving shelter
everywhere, but I am afraid there will be some pains when
the fruit gets ripe. The insect life here is extraordinary,
every kind of creeping, crawling, or buzzing thing. Huge
ants have the most peculiar roads sometimes up the side of
a house. Dragonflies of every hue swing over the stagnant
pools while in the meadows a perfect host of many
coloured butterflies brighten the endless green of the vines.
The mulberry trees are being just striped of their leaves for
the silk worms and look very for long, but the silk worms
must be fed and thousands of them help to keep the Italian
ladies in clothing and employment. There are no fish in the
rivers; I suppose they run too fast. There are some awfully
good gardens here, mostly great masses of rambler roses,
with a number of common roses to fill up. The cultivation
of garden flowers of our kind is unknown, but of course
everything is sacrificed to the all conquering vine. On the
savage pine woods of Asiagio I came on an English wild
rose growing in the heart of a great rock. The people make
themselves fairly comfortable in the plains but one is
surprised at the vast number of cripples about. However
there are very few beggars and everyone seems to work.
The cattle are fine. All the cows go out in the morning with

****

Letter 38 (continued)

their bells and very picturesque it is, the first time, but being wakened every morning gets a bit tiresome and one then notices that most of the bells are cracked and out of tune. The crops are magnificent. Three crops of hay are taken off the water meadows, which are irrigated from the rivers. The rivers have all artificial beds high above the fields. *Mealies* grow everywhere, and form the chief crop. It's a fine sight to see the bullock teams bringing in the great loads of hay which are brought down the mountain slopes on sledges drawn by women, a great institution which keeps them busy and gives them no time for votes.

Ettrick – River in the Scottish Borders
Mealies – Maize

****

****

Letter 39

All well yet. Its very hot and mosquitoes make life a burden. I have been knocking about a good deal and have been some time on a large lake here. It's a great sight to see the thunderstorms at night. The jugged edges of the great mountains round are lit up by continuous lightening and the waves soon rise to quite a respectable size. Tennison wrote some rather gushy poetry and has a marble tablet inscribed with his effort in the village. I was in one village where never kilt was seen before. The whole place turned out to see this unusual sight and I never was so embarrassed. Although it was Sunday, and I deplore Sunday drinking, we rushed into an *Alliergo* to get a little courage to get back to the boat. With the help of a few mild Italian beers we got through, but it was a trying time. There is a fine old coliseum in Verona. It's not a bad town but electric cars etc make it a little difficult to reconcile the unpleasantness which the *Capulets and Montagues* used to cause. The big towns are very much the same, contrasts of white and black, glaring sunlit streets and cool dark shadows below endless arches, black interiors, shuttered, lifeless, everything asleep. Padova is not bad; smashed a bit as all towns are bound to be now. I am going to Venice on Sunday and will write you of my impressions there. There is a great deal to see in the towns and some of the monasteries are fine, the pictures and wood carving particularly. I don't know that I care for the Italian interpretation of the somewhat fleshy large footed apostles. Also you get rather a glut of them. But I must say the crucifixion delineations are magnificent after the

****

Letter 39 (continued)

absolutely dreadful figures in France, and without going into the ghastly details so beloved by the French, in nearly every case show a great nobility of conception and invariably get the atmosphere of pathos and this is to many people the dominate emotion. But give me the mountains, the endless pines, the cool winds and the great banks of wild flowers; I was taking a walk round the line the other morning at sun rise when we saw a fox in the no mans land. I regret to say some unfortunate Austrians, who had been there since the offensive, were the attraction. My friend shot him and we slipped out and got it. It had a splendid skin but there was no way of keeping it. There are little owls here and the men have some young ones they are trying to tame. We got a shell in our hut the other day and many good boys went west and lie in our little graveyards which will relapse when the last gun fires to the eternal silence which wind and trees hardly break. Well, well perhaps the QUAAC's will never get up here, they would soon break the silence. Now I haven't much more to say. We have lost one of the coy pups and that has shed rather a gloom on the community. (You never let me know if you invested that money for me, the £250 I gave you). Alec Ross has got his promotion to corporal, he is a good lad. Give my respects to all, Rankine, Annie and the rest and good luck to you all with the coupons.

Alliergo – local tavern
Capulets and Montagues – Names of characters which dominated the story of 'Romeo and Juliet with their jealous feud

****

****

Letter 40

All well yet. Glorious weather. Of course we get the most terrific thunder storms but they help to cool the place down a bit. I'm living in a great convent at present. These old monks here know how to do themselves well. The dining room is splendid. All around the walls are fine panels of polished wood with the graining all matched. Marble has been used. Above is a network of the most intricate carving in wood. On the walls are hung numerous pictures of opulent looking apostles with more than a suspicion of a hankering after vino, invariably flat footed. In fact all the priests here are away at the feet. This depressing defect seems to have run in the Italian clerical circles from the earliest times. In my room is a perfectly awful picture, revolting in its realism and beautiful execution of some unfortunate saint being skinned alive. From the expression of his face he does not seem to be much annoyed at losing his property in this violent way but no doubt he is being reconciled to his loss by two over developed females with totally inadequate wings which are standing by enjoying the fun. It makes me creep to look at it. I sent you two jars from Venice. Very interesting and novel but a little disappointing. The canals and lagoons are crowded now, not with gay Venetians in gondolas, but by steam launches, motor boats, etc, and the sanitary condition of many of the back canals leave much to be desired. St Marks is well worth seeing but is spoiled to the casual visitor by the enormous mass of detail. Titian, Tintoretto and other great artists have given of their best and the result is confusing. The bulk of the decoration is in mosaic and this is done in glass, gilded. To our northern eyes the decoration of a church in the style of a first rate gin palace is a bit disconcerting. The guides are a public nuisance and seem to take a great delight in pointing out that nearly everything has been pinched from Alexandria or other probable unoffending places. The glorious singing of the gondoliers is a myth. The only one who sang was our own one and we had the greatest difficulty stopping that in order to restore the peace of the night. His effort was a ribald song on the late General Cadrona and was no doubt induced by us paying him something on account in the afternoon and the presence of an Aliergo. The whole country is now covered by the extra ordinary growing vegetation and the grapes are well formed on the vines. They don't look too healthy to me but I suppose they're all right. The insect life unhappily now is at its height. It's rather interesting that where I am staying was once Napoleons' head quarters and I regret to say that when he left he thoroughly looted the whole concern. War was war in these happy days and not just dreary fighting like it is now. The old priest here speaks French a bit and would be quite a decent looking old boy with a good wash and a shave. Well I wish it were finished. You must not let *Rankine* go. You will need him for the potato crop at Galahill and the garden. It would be just a great a loss to let the garden away as to send him on the land. The garden is all productive now and must be kept up. Well now I haven't much more to say. Good luck Willie

Rankine – Minnie's Gardener / Hired Help
****

Letter 41

6 / 9 / 18

All well yet. The weather is still very hot. We are in another convent – the country is covered with them. The place has been made for hot weather and is in squares with arched passages, always cool. It is all white and the courtyards are exquisite, especially in the moonlight, as the simplicity of the whole effect gives the shadows a clear cut, definite background for the white pillars and arches. A great tower above dwarfs the whole design and this only adds to the delicacy of the whole effect. You find this very often in the Italian squares as at St Marks, and until you get used to it, and understand, the towers look out of place and hideous. St Marks is a fairy land of detail. Pavements, pillars, ceilings vie with each other in a riot of colour; the general effect is gold and scarlet. We had a different guide, a seedy creature who needed a shave badly. He spoke English well, however, and evidently shared the general contempt for priests which is obviously shown here. In the Titian Chapel, where there is a virgin by some other great artist with an imaginative mind, we found the sacrament being adminersed. This Virgin is clad in the magnificent clothes of the Borgia period and is covered with jewels guaranteed by the management to be real; a large audience of women were present with one or two lost looking old men, obviously brought there by their wives, and looking hot and bored. The ladies all use fans. The young priest who officiated, knocked the thing through at a tremendous rate, it was getting near lunch time. I regret to say that my kilt proved more than a counter attraction to the transubstantiation which was going on. Even the priest

Letter 41 (continued)

slowed down a bit eventually with gratification at having a few men in the audience. This, however, didn't suit our guide who, when he found we wouldn't walk through the service, and listen to his remark on the alter which in cold blood he proposed doing, told us sulkily to wait two minutes and it would be finished. He then managed to catch the lagging priests eye by loud coughing, and treated him to such a ferocious scowl that the unhappy man got on with it with renewed vigour and finished well within the two minutes promised by the guide. The Venetian Contadine are very graceful, beautiful necks and small heads, black hair predominating, with red a good second. Their carriage is good but they have bad feet and ankles. This is just opposite to the French girls. The long fringed shawls they wear draped round them are very effective as they are invariably black and are arranged to show glimpses of splendid colours, colours which beneath our skies would clash, but within the deep blue here, with the white houses and golden domes, scarlet roofs and endless glowing wisteria, they seem quietly suitable. The signorina's have all gone. It's a bit too near the line now and the great places are shut up, the shutters are closed behind the wrought ironwork and the paint is rotting on the walls. There is always a queer feeling in an uninhabited town. In Nervesa, and some of the towns we have gone into near the front, it is a bad thing to go about in the moonlight and see the half open doors, the swinging shutters, the litter on the floors, half finished meals, broken toys, with here and there the twisted equipment and bloody bandages, where some poor creature has been hastily

****

Letter 41 (continued)

attended to. Fire flies still light the overgrown, trampled gardens, littered with the tins and refuse which go with armies. Here and there are roofless blackened ruin give reason for the hurried flight tenanted by the rats. There is no silence at night here as there is a misguided beetle who persist in rubbing his hind legs together producing a sort of musical scraping noise. The frogs also croak all night and there is the endless scuffling and squeaking of rats. However, you get used to anything, and any continuous noise is better than the nightingales. The vines are now in full fruit, purple amongst the green, ready to give socks to unhappy tommies who indulge in them. Well I've nothing much more to tell you so good luck. W

****

Officers 2nd Batallion (William Neilson Brown pictured from row 2nd left)

****

Letter 42

I am sorry I did not write sooner but I did my best. I'm very well and not injured in any way. My knees are all small cuts but the shrapnel is out but it will take a little time to heal as the wounds are septic. What a glorious fight it was. We lined up about 8 o'clock at night and then lay till 5.30 next morning under a heavy rain of shells. Gas too and trench mortars, and every kind of unpleasantness. Well in the early morning darkness we crept towards the river up to the knees in water under cover of high brushwood. Just as dawn broke we came on them. The river is waist high and very swift, but we charged through onto the machine guns which were now kicking up a devil of a shindy. I was first over the river but you needn't say this. We cut the wire under heavy fire and soon had the machine gunners killed. After that it was a picnic. We fought them through a thick wood, hunting them out and then had as pretty a bit of village fighting as one would wish. After that it was merely a matter of chasing with here and there a stout lot to reduce in some house. I never saw the boys fight like it. My coy, took over 400 prisoners including a brigadier with his staff. Well I hope it will all help to finish the war and that is the main thing. I suppose winter will be very nearly on you now. I was very near leave and may get it when I go back this all depends on my knees. We lost our commanding officer early in the stunt and some very good friends of mine as well but this is inevitable and happily has not the effect that such tragic things would have in peace times. My happy trip to Rome

****

Letter 42 (continued)

was cut short, hard lines, for I was just beginning to understand and appreciate the spirit of the place. One has to have a proper guide, a man who can appreciate the beauty of objects, whether views or buildings, and pick out and contrast those beauties without prejudice as to age. I was lucky to have such a guide and was just setting off with him on a tour to Naples and Pompeii when the fateful telegram arrived. Genoa is a fine town and I will have a description of it when I can get up. I was sorry to hear of Max. *Gala* has given well to the war but how could anyone keep out of it. Good luck for the present, I have got off very lightly and will soon be back at the Austrians again. Peace should come now, we can only hope so.

Gala – shortened word for the town of Galashiels, Scottish Borders

****

Letter 43

10 / 12 / 18

All well yet but very tired of it all now the war seems to be over. It's very cold but we are fairly comfortable and everything is going fairly well. Of course we are trying to educate the men but its uphill work after such a long time without any need for it. We are billeted in the hills again. Some splendid views in the morning and at night. Now the dead leaves are off the vines they don't look so bad. Of course the regularity of the trees which support the vines are difficult to appreciate after our woods and the terraces on the hills give a patchwork effect. The great effects are got by the immensity of the plains which stretch in to the blue haze which always softens the landscape. Every now and then we get one of these intensely clear days when the Alps seem just outside the house and every little white house on the lower slopes are clear and distinct. We had an inspection by the King of Italy – a cold affair. This is as about all the recognition we have got for having broken the Piave. Well I don't know if I'll be home for Xmas. I might, but don't have any hopes at present. Well I haven't much to write about now but peace makes up for everything. The only thing is to put the huns out. We don't trust their revolutions.
W

Sergeants of A Company, who were in final attack, June 26th 1918, on Piave

****

Letter 44

All well yet. I've quite recovered and my knee is now all right. I had about five cuts but only one bit in. I don't suppose there's any harm in telling you about the Piave stunt. Well, one afternoon we got word that we were 'going over' and at 6pm we marched off. Up the long straight roads we marched bumping through the traffic which was congested beyond description, lorries with ammunition, staff cars, motorcycles of every description, guns great and small, pontoons to make the river bridges, Italians, British, refugees, all seen in the headlights of some fast car and lost immediately in the night. Away to the right a terrific shindy was going on over a bombing aeroplane in the distance the white signal lights marked out our destination. We marched until we were about done, in silence, and with no smokes, and at last came to our destination close to the Piave. It had now started to rain and we spent the night lying in the wet grass beneath the grateful shade of rows of half dead vines. All next day we lay there hardly daring to move for if an enemy aeroplane had spotted us, and we were two divisions he would have given us a particularly hot reception. Well it rained all that night and all the next day and raised the river so much that the attack was put off. I was right down at the river before I heard that it was put off and we were pretty sick because you have more anxiety in the hours before an attack than any other time and it was all to do over again. Next day was fine and was appreciated as we spent a wretched night, wet through, couldn't get a smoke, and little food and that

****

Letter 44 (continued)

cold. Well at 6pm at night we started off with guides down to the river. An island had been captured in the middle and we were going to attack from that, wading the further stream. It was a very dark night and it was a nervous business. When we came to the river bank the engineers had a foot bridge constructed to the island and over we went. Now the island is not what we understand by that name. On these rivers it is simply shingle covered with little trees about the height of your head. There are half a dozen little streams flowing through this and a more confusion place in the day time can hardly be imagined. You can understand what it was like at night. The whole island was about 5 km long by 3 wide. We stumbled through the bushes and got into battle line behind a 'bund' this is a long bank to protect the country from flooding. It is necessary on all these snow fed streams. In about ten minutes time the most awful uproar got up. Our barrage had opened. The whole sky was lit up with the shaded orange flashes of the big guns, and the Austrian was not slow to reply. We were given a dressing down the like of I have never had since Bullecourt shrapnel was buzzing over and a particularly unpleasant trench mortar which could just hardly reach us, but kept you in constant apprehension. The usual assortment of scrap iron was forth coming and a little gas. Then it started to rain. We had only the faintest idea of the direction of the enemy or the distance to him. We did know that he was ready and waiting for us with every kind of unpleasantness in stock and so ended this perfect day. My silver watch and cigarette case were absolutely black with the shell fumes on this 'bund'. At

Letter 44 (continued)

5.30 we started going forward through the wet bushes. It was pitch black, and you could hear the little groups moving all around, but see almost no one. We seemed to go for miles. As a matter of fact it was little more than a kilometre. Over two little streams which at the time we thought must be the Piave, until at last we came out on a stream as broad as the Ettrick about 4 feet deep on the shallows and running fifteen miles an hour. At the same instant the machine guns lashed the water into spray and the first stage of the work was done. My coy was up against the Austrians in good formation, I saw men falling in the river so made a dash across with my servant and got over first of the battalion. It was great luck. The men came cheering after and we cut the wire under their noses. They were so frightened with our noise they left the gun in front of us and I got through the wire and got a rifle and bayonet from a man whose kilt was caught in the wire and rushed round the back of the Austrian gun that was holding us up. I jumped into the post and the two gunners were sitting with their backs to me serving their gun to the end. One of them was a strong faced Austrian, the other a young weedy looking fellow. He took open his tunic and kept touching the hole where the bullet came through his breast and whimpered. I gave him all the cigarettes I had but we had to hurry on for the men were streaming over now and there was much to do. The river lines were broken but about three hundred yards behind them were other lines constructed in another bund. Connecting these two were parallel bands of wire to keep you straight up to the

Letter 44 (continued)

machine guns. We cut the wire rushed these defences, and were masters of them in about half an hour. It was very pretty fighting as the place was thickly wooded and two officers were killed here by snipers. This sniper was in a high branch and when we located him we fired three or four Lewis guns into his perch till he came dropping out head downwards, holding on with one hand for a last instant while the merciless guns roared on. The Austrians were absolutely beaten now and surrendered, white faced, hands up, from every hole and corner. You couldn't kill them they were such miserable sites. We came out of the wood into the village and here there was some hard fighting. The village was very much knocked about hardly a house had a roof but snipers fired from the windows and machine guns sprayed the roads. The church, a mere shell, was strongly held. We got two hundred prisoners from it but we fought them out of it and pressed on. The fighting now was quite different. Each isolated house was a garrison and had to be surrounded and rushed. We got four hundred prisoners from three of these houses. The Austrians fired the machine guns from the windows but we split into four parties, crept up to near as possible and charged the house. Whenever we charged they surrendered and it was comical to see them coming running out of the doors and jumping from the windows and a mad effort to surrender quickly. Sometimes one little JOCK moved off with 200 Austrians behind him, their only guide, counsellor and friend. At last we came to their brigade headquarters and this was some prize. About twelve officers and two hundred and fifty men we got, their

Letter 44 (continued)

brigadier himself and all his staff. By a bit of luck he came out the door I rushed and I got him. He gave me his sword and automatic pistol I couldn't bring the sword but have the sword knot. I took his bugle from his trumpeter and will bring them all home. By this time it was getting late and word had just come that our commanding officer had been killed in the village and the adjutant badly wounded, so we started to make a defence line. My knees were beginning to give me news of themselves and on examination I found them pretty bad but never noticed it before, though of course we all got a terrible fright with the shell which did burst not more than five yards off. In these cases you are so stunned and sick and so glad to be alive that minor injuries are overlooked. I stayed in a house all night and in about three hours could not walk but got some tea and with a rifle beside you felt fit for any wretched Austrian. In the night we had three alarms with terrific uproars of machine gun and rifle fire but they came to nothing. In the room I was in were four wounded Austrians poor wretches, two died during the night, and we were thankful to get their blankets for it was bitterly cold. Another became delirious in the early morning he cried some name out and sang little German songs. He was a decent looking middle aged man and I gave him some water, but he would hardly drink and cried unceasingly the one word, no doubt someone dear to him. He got hold of my hand and wouldn't let go. I had to wrench it away he seemed frightened to die, so lonely. Well, the next day I came over the Piave on a stretcher, down to Genoa and so ended the battle. The colonel recommended a bar to the

****

Letter 44 (continued)

MC but it didn't come through. There were so many and they all did well. Now this letter is absolutely confidential only for the family. I have every hope of being back for Xmas and expect to start next Sunday.

****

Very cold winds yet but dry now and some faint signs of spring. I am alright, and we have been through it again and the regiments did splendidly. I had to go up and take over command of two coys for a short time. We are resting now in a great expanse of woods and hills. You can hardly imagine the assault. The village lay on the top of a long slope and we lay in position on the opposite slope. It was moonlight and very cold and clear. After an eternity of waiting the dawn crept in and suddenly a signal gun rang out. Then the deluge, nothing could be heard but the shells swishing over and the roll of the guns. As the sun rose red over the village everything was coloured a rosy pink and the flashes of the bursts made a magnificent picture, the shattered houses being veiled by a haze of drifting smoke. As the light cleared the long lines of men could be seen walking quietly forward through the bursts, German by now, and disappearing over the ridge behind the village. Back down the slopes came the little dots; walking wounded, orderlies and carrying parties moving over the great slopes made a scene of orderly confusion. That's all now, no glorious charging in magnificent uniforms, just kill and be killed by science; and God help the German machine gunners for they are 'for it'. They lay in the sunken road twisted into absurd attitudes, fine big men, finished with it. Let's hope it won't last much longer, another winter will be awful and it's difficult to see how it can end. Send me a parcel now and then but not expensive ones, cakes, mealy puddings, etc, are the best things for we are not within reach of any food now. Also send Keating's the lice are awful and make your life a torment. This regiment is the 92nd, you asked about that.

THE LIST.

(This list read is the list of campaigns
with the official names of battles and
their boundaries, which are groups of
battles are in italics)

1.—FRANCE AND FLANDERS.

1914.
Mons.—Aug. 23-24.
Le Cateau.—Aug. 26.
The Marne.—1914, Sept. 7-10.
The Aisne.—1914, Sept. 12-15.
La Bassee.—Oct. 10-Nov. 2.
Messines.—1914, Oct. 12-Nov. 2.
Armentieres.—Oct. 13-Nov. 2.
YPRES, 1914.
Oct. 19-Nov. 22.

1915.
Neuve Chapelle.—Mar. 10-13.
Ypres.—1915, April 22-May 25.
Aubers Ridge.—May 9.
Festubert.—May 15-25.
Loos.—Sept. 25-Oct. 8.

1916.
Mount Sorrel.—June 2-13.
The Somme.—1916, July 1-Nov. 18.

1917.
Arras.—1917, April 9-May 4.
Bullecourt.—May 3-17.
Hill 70.—Aug. 15-25.
Messines.—1917, June 7-14.
Ypres.—1917, July 31-Nov. 10.
Cambrai.—1917, Nov. 20-Dec. 3.

1918.
First Somme.—1918, Mar. 21-April 5.
The Lys.—April 29.
The Aisne.—1918, May 27-June 6.
The Marne.—1918, July 20-Aug. 2.
Amiens.—Aug. 8-11.
Second Somme.—1918, Aug. 21-Sept. 3.
Second Arras.—1918, Aug. 26-Sept. 3.
Hindenburg Line.—Sept. 12-Oct. 9.
Ypres.—1918, Sept. 28-Oct. 2.
Courtrai.—Oct. 14-19.
The Selle.—Oct. 17-25.
Valenciennes.—Nov. 1-2.
The Sambre.—Nov. 4.

2.—ITALY.

1917.
10th Isonzo.—May 12-June 8.
11th Isonzo.—Aug. 17-Sept. 12.
12th Isonzo.—Oct. 24-Nov. 12.
The Piave.—June 15-24.
Vittorio Veneto.—Oct. 24-Nov. 4.

3.—MACEDONIA.
Doiran, 1917.—Apr. 24, 25-May 8, 9.
Doiran, 1918.—Sept. 18, 19.

4.—DARDANELLES.
Helles.—Apr. 25-June 6.
Anzac.—Apr. 25-June 30.
Suvla.—Aug. 6, 21.

5.—Sudan (against Darfur), 1916.
6.—Western Frontier (Egypt against Senussi), 1915-1916.
7.—Eastern Frontier, Egypt, and Palestine

1916.
Rumani.—Aug. 4-5.
1917.
First Gaza.—Mar. 26-27.
Second Gaza.—Apr. 17-19.
Third Gaza.—Oct. 27-Nov. 7.
Nebi Samwil.—Nov. 17-24.
Jerusalem.—Dec. 26-30.
Jaffa.—Dec. 21-22.

1918.
Megiddo.—Sept. 19-25.

8.—Hejaz operations, 1914-1918.
9.—Southern Arabia, 1914-1918.
10.—Mesopotamia.
Shaiba.—Apr. 12-14, 1915.
Kut.—1915, Sept. 28.
Ctesiphon.—Nov. 22-24, 1915.
Defence of Kut.—Dec. 7, 1915-April 28, 1916.
Kut.—1917, Jan. 9—Feb. 24.
Sharquat.—Oct. 28-30, 1918.

Newspaper cutting with list of battles during WW1

****

Letter 46

All going well yet. It's the rainy season just now. But between the rains we have these perfect days of sunshine when it's never too hot. In Scotland our spring runs into summer far too quickly. Spring in Italy is perfect but the summer is very trying to northern people. Strange isn't it that our nation stands extremes so well, even better than the peoples who are accustomed to them. Last year we were in the Alps up to the knees in melting snow and wet through with the drip of the endless forests of pines. We have now comfortable huts and every convenience, but then we had little canvas shelters and no fires during the day. But of course the summer on the hills was splendid. The flowers and butterflies were alone a pleasure and the pines gave that solemn shade which no other woods can. Of course we were above the clouds and that was a decided drawback as many days we were shrouded with the great mists as thick as a London fog with intense bursts of sunshine in between. Necessity makes you acquainted with strange bed fellows. One of the wonders of Italy is the conservation of water and the gravel brought down by the floods. The beds of the rivers have been raised above the level of the plains and have high artificial banks, sometimes thirty feet. Sluices in these banks irrigate the whole country, and water meadows on either side of the streams on which two, and sometimes three crops of hay is harvested. Along the irrigation ditches, endless lines of willows and other trees supply the brushwood which is used for fuel and between them lie the long rows of mulberries and vines. All the dry banks and roadsides have dense masses of the acacia and the effect produced is an

****

Letter 46 (continued)

astonishing mass of foliage dividing a great chess board.
The vines run north and south as a rule and this has often
proved very useful in determining positions. The acacia,
though a very free grower has the most brutal thorns, often
an inch long, which give a poisonous cut, no scratch I can
tell you, and the kilt is not the best dress for getting
through these thickets. The bark is poisonous and we have
lost many horses through eating it, though strangely
enough Italian horses seem to eat it with impunity. This is
the land of queer dogs. You never see two the same, and
you never seem to finish seeing an uglier one than the last
one you thought was the ugliest. (Rather involved sentence
that). They are all very good natured and rather very
cowardly and about the best 'scroungers' you could
imagine. They belong to the leisured classes, however, not
like their French relations. No wheels for butter or carts as
in Belgium. A great lot more motor drivers and the VAD's
have arrived. A poor officer I was with fell down on the
road with a severe heart attack the other night and when
we stopped an ambulance to get him home, the driver was
heard to mutter, I wish so many people wouldn't get drunk
at night. So that shows how women jump at conclusions,
generally wrong ones. I took some photos of the Dago
munitions girls the other day but don't know how they will
come out. They get up regardless and posed with much
giggling and nose powdering. They haven't votes here and
that's one good thing, and this is one of the few things in
which the Italians are ahead of us. It's as cold as an east
wind day at home today. The winds from the sea generally
are very cold and bring rain. Of course we are on a high

****

Letter 46 (continued)

plateau here. It's a pull up all the way from Genoa, and in spite of the heat there is still snow on the hills around. We are planting potatoes and other vegetables now, the 'Austriches' supplying the labour, but I hope I'll not be at the harvest. I hope to be back June or July, you never can tell. I hope you are all well and that the weather is improving. It will soon be time for weeding and the garden again, it will be armistice work now. There's no better fun for earnest war workers than weeding – exercise, duty to the country, and amusement mixed.

****

****

Letter 47

Well, everything is alright. The snow only lasted two days. High winds from the sea with showers of rain, but warmth and plenty sun. The trees are coming out and everything looks fresher for the wintry spell. Yesterday we got one of these days when the atmosphere was so clear that the details of the hills were visible, all the little wooded ravines, tiny clumps of white and red houses, and on the tops of the hills, great monasteries and churches, round the white wall grow great dark Cyprus trees and round the spire cluster the bewildering number of little roofs at all angles. It's a strange custom building these places on the hilltops as the food and fuel have to be taken up by pack animals. One particularly inaccessible monastery near here has little shrines at every corner of the zig zag road that leads through the vines to the brushwood on above that to the bear rocks on the crest. You are supposed to go up on your hands and knees pausing at the shrines for a moment's prayer, and so wiping out any arrears of sin which may be debited to you at the time. From the steepness of the path and the stones I would deduct that Nero himself would come out of the trip with something in credit. Well there's not much to write you about. On a clear day the Alps stand out in the far distance white, clear cut, pink in the glorious sunsets. The sun rises are disappointing. Perhaps it is the want of the birds and wildlife which seem so tame in these early hours. The sea at Genoa gives a variety to the scenery. Mountains, long rolling hills, the plains, and the sea all within sight. Whenever possible I take a trip to Genoa for the change.
Let me know when you get the book I sent you. I think you

****

Letter 47 (continued)

will find it very interesting. I will be sending you all my winter clothing which you can keep for my return as everything is dear now and it will come in handy. I'm glad I've got such good suits already at home. I won't require anything and I expect to be back at the end of June for good. The garden will soon be beginning to green now. It should be improving every year now, but of course when a place is let away, you have to improve it very slowly. I got your letter alright and enjoyed it. It's rather a monotonous life here. In fact if it wasn't for the walks I would be pretty fed up. The government appears to be releasing raw material very slowly. I hope you can get wool soon. It seems very short sighted policy to keep back all the manufacturers of the country. Expect it is because the huge number of officials who will lose their jobs if these control ministries are shut up. There's rather much Wilson just now. Everybody's getting a bit fed up on all the talk of the Americas noble part. The world of course knows that the 'Yankees and Dagos' won the war so why do they still persist in blustering about their 'divine ,mission' or 'sacred trust' and whining for a few crumbs of praise over their 'patriotic fervour' or unity of 'righteous purpose'. Perhaps the quiet noticed homecoming of the Gordon's to Aberdeen may be as dignified as the noisy flag wagging long silent hand shaking melodramas which appear to go on in New York. However, these things have got to be put up with I suppose for the sake of our 'Gallant Allies', but to some of us the description of an average American welcome brings home the real horrors of war. Well well. Perhaps we are a bit tired of it all, and enthusiasm over

Letter 47 (continued)

these things seems to grate after what we have gone through. The term 'hero' has become too cynical now that the main thing is to get shut of those qualified for this description as cheaply as possible. I must thank you for the suit lengths, they couldn't be better. I have always been very fond of these home spuns, liked them better than Harris, which is rather thick. I've had the first warm night last night. The warm damp smell of spring, from the newly ploughed land and bursting trees, you can almost see the leaves growing and certainly a difference every morning. I suppose you have had your share of the 'flu'. We've had a fare share and some deaths. The Austrians have had a few also. They are a good race, well set up men, and now they have good rations, stout and prosperous looking. They have a good string band with instruments provided and seem happy. They play football also and feeling runs so high at these matches that when the Austrians beat the Hungarians, a free fight followed, and now each nation is kept at opposite sides of the field. They are friendly to us and are streets better than the Dagos. In fact, if they had been fed and led they would have put up a defence which no Dago could have touched. It's a marvel considering the condition they were in, how well they did when they crossed the Piave. I hope you are well and that things are going well.

W

I'm in charge of a camp of girls now, 500 Italian munitions workers. There's a big hospital here full of WAAC's and VAD's and motor drivers so Wuffie will agree it is a dangerous locality. We have a fine contessa to keep the Dago girls in order. Plenty nose powdering going on in working hours. Plenty chatting and when you go in suddenly plenty fancy work shoved under the tables, plenty buzzing.

W

****

Years after returning home from War Major Brown wrote the following account of the 'Forcing of Piave'

****

The 20ᵗʰ Brigade on the River Piave, October, 1918 by W. Neilson Brown

The forcing of the river Piave opened the way to the victory of Vittorio Veneto, with the collapse and ending of the Austrian empire. The greatest gamble of the war, dependant on the weather in October, the very element of chance appealed to a sporting people and all ranks approved of the attempt.

We knew the Piave well, and its moods from the slopes of the Montello we had watched its flood and fall through months of duty in the line.

But the hard bitten company commanders had few illusions left, few enthusiasms. War was just a dreary trade, and any change from the present was bound to be for the worse. After Loos, Bullecourt, and Ypres, little enthusiasm could be raised for 'action' apart from its interlude in the weary monotony.

The 7ᵗʰ division were billeted in Treviso, an abandoned town of much bombing and few cigarettes. Two nights had been spent at the railway station, with the unusual accompaniment of heavy rain, unloading vast quantities of ammunition for the various guns. Twice nightly the dreary business was enlivened by hostile aeroplanes.

No doubt we were inured to sudden death, and reasonably fatalistic, but to the shelter from anti aircraft splinters beneath a truck of gas and high explosive shells during a bombing raid is certainly trying.

Whisky and cigarettes were short, and as these might reasonably be termed necessitates, life was extremely unpleasant.

Night time in an empty town is no experience for the nervous. Treviso was not so bad while the troops were about; a few 'Alliergo's' were open, with 'red ink' and vile brandy to suit mans different tastes, but after 'lights out' the queer brooding mystery of empty houses, with the sinister blackness beneath the arched sidewalks, kept one in the centre of the street through a vague uneasiness.

Nervesa, on the banks of Piave, was a better example. The Italian soldiers had thoroughly looted the place in their rout from Caparetto. To walk through the streets in the full light of the moon was an experience to those who thought that life's emotions were ended as an entertainment. The half open doors, the curtained windows, the litter garden patches, all spoke of human life and company. But the silence was dreadful; not the voice of a child, not the bark of a dog, not the rumble of a cart; just that deep sinister silence brooding overall, making the sudden hoot of an owl or the rush of a rat in the discarded tins a thing of nervous startling. Perhaps it was the Border Scotch blood, but I was always glad to get out of Nervesa and up on the open hills.

The order to 'fall in', in fighting order, was therefore almost welcome. True, the company commander from being worried to death with endless orders would now be worried to Hades, but once on the move one could ignore the bulk of the brigade and divisional literature.

Of course it rained, this was now essential to major schemes of operation, and we trudged up the road in that queer acceptance of circumstances when the worst had come and all 'grousing' stops.

At length we took to the fields in single file, wading a

muddy ditch and ploughing through knee high grass that held the rain like a sponge. We halted at a high hedge of neglected overgrown vines, and we were informed that this was our billet.

In the old days of 'The Salient' or 'Beaumont Hammel', the vine hung ditch would have been looked on as a 'Hotel Splendide' in the way of accommodation. But our sojourn in Italy had raised the standard of living considerably; all ranks viewed their sleeping quarters in dismay.

Italian bivouacs were issued, soaking little patches of cloth hung on two sticks, and soon the battalion had settled down in the surprising way of infantrymen.

The Italian bivouacs might give reasonable accommodation to a fair sized dog; there are no 'cruelty' officers in Italy. Three huge 'Jocks' were expected to share a bivouac, and managed to do so. The quarter master, with his usual tact giving out each bivouac would hold four, the three ultimate occupants imagined that they had any amount of room.

The next day dawned in bright sunshine and all discomforts were forgotten. No one was allowed to leave the shelter of the vines, to avoid aeroplane observation, and as the 'foot' soldier preferred sitting still to anything else, this was no hardship.

Towards evening we had an excellent entertainment. Three Austrian aeroplanes appeared and attacked a British captive balloon. The 'balloonatics' (this was no misnomer in the late stages of the war) hopped out 'multo prompto', and their parachutes functioning were soon on their way to safety. The Austrian 'planes' fired the captive balloon; but the last struck the wire rope with its wing. The pilot jumped out, and his parachute also worked.

For a moment, three parachutes, a burning balloon, and a crashing aeroplane, were in the air at once. This may be some kind of war record; thousands of men saw and must remember the scene.

The next day all company commanders joined a 'Cook's Tour' arranged by the Brigade. We had only a vague idea of the scheme; the river would be crossed in boats, a previous practice at Treviso made this part certain. The practice had been greatly enjoyed, a welcome change from company and army drill, with plenty of the sitting about that infantry like. But to the thinking the overloaded boats looked extremely dangerous, even on the still stream. However, the Sergeant Major fell heavily in the river, the only casualty, so the day ended a complete and happy memory.

With this knowledge, an inspection of the island of Papadopoli was far from reassuring. The river bed at this point seemed a mile across. Mostly white shingle, torn from the Alps when melting snow filled this wide expanse with rushing water, the long island lay low and black on the white level plain, impossible to approach, impregnable to attack. The whole island seemed covered with dense brushwood above which towered a few trees.

Small streams wandered down the wide bed of shingle, but the main river was on our side, close up to our bank; it was obvious that the fast running stream of icy temperature was no place for boating.

The Brigade Major gave us the usual vague little lecture. Only one thing was definite, the 22nd Brigade would conduct the regatta and capture the island. A bridge would be built for the 20th Brigade to which we belonged. The news was most grateful; we viewed the island with a new enthusiasm, and especially the far bank of the river that would be our objective. It was a relief to get out of the boat business; the Scotch have never been a seafaring nation.

After two nights beneath the vine we were off at last,

found the bridge as promised, crossed to the captured island and started the long trudge to our position.

Of course it rained, and was a particularly dark night. Even though the guide was my best *Subaltern*, who had passed the whole day on the island, that plunge into the wilderness of brushwood was most anxious. In single file, at a snail's pace to prevent straggling, we mauled our way through the soaking scrub, waded small streams and muddy ditches and toiled over abandoned fields of knee high grass. Twice we crossed trenches, stumbling through the wire and litter of rifles and helmets; it was queer to feel the old sour smell of 'Fritz' in these places, quite different to our own.

At last we emerged on a wide open space of rank grass, our destination. The company was collected and thrown in artillery formation; the rain increased to torrents, the usual rumour was disposed of that half the company was lost, the Sergeant Major reported that the spare ammunition could not be found, the men no doubt started eating up their emergency rations and throwing away bombs, rockets and aeroplane flares. And so, in the accepted way of the British soldier, in spite of science, discipline, orders and war offices, we stripped to the good old rifle and bayonet and waited for the assault.

Up to this time the night had been a model of peace, not a shell disturbed the sinister quiet; but something annoyed 'Jerry', something woke him up, and from that time we received a constant stream of assorted shells from every callibre of Austrian gun. The ground was soft and little harm was done, but when shrapnel started the company was moved behind a high bank.

A Brigade runner arrived; these pests could always find you, to ask if we were in touch with the Italians on the right. We were not. No trace of the Italians could be found as orderlies sent out in the wilderness simply disappeared for good. The 'runner' was misdirected back by the Sergeant Major, a man of fine perception, with this information. If the runner was lost there would be no more annoyance. A dug out full of Italians was ultimately found; the language question as usual made things hopeless. But they were there, and a runner was sent off to say we were in touch. They may have been fugitive Austrians for all we knew, the uniforms much the same, but it ended the bother. Zero hour arrived at last. We rose and moved forward; in the dim light there was one glimpse of the line of men plunging in the brushwood and the affair was in the hands of the Gods.

By crossing the watercourses at right angles, an idea impressed on all ranks, really wonderful direction was kept. We were well ahead of the schedule time when the brushwood suddenly ended, and we were on the far river bank. And a more unpleasant place for war purposes could hardly be imagined. Fifty yards of flat white shingle lay to the swift black stream; the high bank beyond was wired and loop holed. The British barrage was landing on this far bank, but after Flanders you could have 'put it in your eye'. According to the time table we should have waited for its lifting, but the enemy machine guns were now clattering from their posts and the air was full of cracking bullets. Men came crashing through the bushes every instant, to find themselves on the open shingle; there was nothing else for it, with a shout we rushed for the stream. The water was waist high and icy cold, but that was nothing with the spray of machine gun bullets as an incentive to speed. Somehow we got through the wire, what infantryman can ever explain how this was done, and running along the back of the bank shot the machine gunners.

The guns were on a projecting corner, and as they ceased

our men poured over scathless and the bank was won. The surprise was complete; the British barrage still slammed amongst us, but the whole Austrian garrison were in their dug outs waiting for its lifting before manning the bank. Gamblers luck indeed, for the casualties were nothing and the position should have been impregnable. On our left, the unfortunate battalion who kept to the time table had stiff opposition and a serious 'cutting up'. We sheltered from our shells, as it was no use going on until the barrage lifted and the whole line would move forward.

The Austrian machine gunners were interesting as totally divergent types. The big man lay on his back, splendidly made, in middle age, with fine clean cut features and a great thin nose. The other was a youth in his 'teens' fair haired with a round stupid face, almost featureless. He sobbed wildly as he pressed his hand to his chest, where the bullet had emerged. It was obviously above the lung and not much harm done; he got the last packet of cigarettes, an impulse that afterwards was deeply regretted. Almost immediately came retribution for the disdaining of the time table. A small British shell landed at my feet; in the soft ground the explosion was nothing. The others escaped scathless, but for an instant I felt a savage sting in my knee. It was nothing; two sharp cuts on the bare leg and a small round hole beside the knee cap. With the excitement of victory it was forgotten in the immediate burst of laughter at the escape.

The barrage had lifted, at least it wasn't bothering us now, so the advance was ordered against a village that loomed through the trees.

We left the crowded dug outs with regret for the 'moppers up'. It always seemed hard that the attackers must leave the prisoners for others, perhaps a complex from the old happy days of loot. No wonder there were hundred year wars when the soldiers kept himself off his conquered foes; successful, front line would never get past the first objective.

The surprise was still complete; with the reduction of one machine gun post the village surrendered and disgorged hundreds of prisoners. The Austrians were weedy and dejected; it was obvious they were half starved. The correct method of surrendering, we soon gathered, was to hurl and steel 'Dolly Varden' into the nearest ditch with a gesture of relief. No doubt it was symbolic, as an exit from the war.

We were pretty safe now, with plenty room behind, and after a rough reorganisation the second phase of the battle commenced. This meant the reduction of isolated farm houses; the element of surprise was over, and some of these long low buildings, with thick walls and numerous small windows, were costly in men and time.

A curious feature of this assault was the extraordinary good humour that prevailed. Not an Austrian was bayoneted; in fact the attitude of the 'Jocks' to the prisoners was almost paternal, as to a misguided child.

But with the stiffened resistance sniping started from the trees, and in this blind country of brushwood and acacia hedges it proved deadly. Two officers and several men were killed before the marksmen could be located on platforms in the high trees. Lewis guns soon ended the annoyance. As we approached a little wood a corporal fell dead, shot through the head. There was no use waiting in the open for another Austrian bullet, so we charged the wood. At its edge and Austrian suddenly dropped from a tree and raced along a deep ditch of holding mud, closely pursued by 'Jock'. Shouts to stop increased if possible his speed. Admitting that pace and mud were against accurate shooting, it seemed incredible that six shots could have missed at a maximum of thirty yards range. When they both stopped through sheer exhaustion the ridiculous side of the thing made the sniper safe.

There was certainly a strong feeling that he should be bayoneted, to square the corporal, but the comic side prevailed.

'I doot ye'll hae to get some practice,' said a big Sergeant, 'it's nae wonder the wars been sic a time in feenishing.'

The answering grins restored the general good humour and we pressed forward to the prize of the day.

This was the Austrian headquarters, a long white farmhouse in a jumble of outbuildings. The first assault failed, with serious casualties. Fortunately our left was well forward, and the next attack on two sides had hardly developed before the surrender.

It was rather comical. Men poured from all kinds of doors, and even threw themselves from the windows. In a few minutes we were a mob, during the confusion two enemy machine guns opened from a neighbouring farm house, fortunately over our heads. The clatter ceased, and the prisoners were sorted out and marched off. Then the staff emerged, with a dozen small boys in uniform, cadets up for experience and instruction. The sight of these frightened youngsters dispelled the last vestige of savagery raised by the snipers.

For the 'Jocks' must have been a terrifying sight to those unused to the kilt. With shaggy goatskin jerkins and steel helmets, a four days beard, and mud and blood from ditch and barbed wire, our once smart battalion was now a ruffianly gang of savage desperados.

The inside of the Headquarters baffles description; every room contained wounded from a chance shell that had pitched in the courtyard. They lay in a confusion of war junk that surprised us, hardened as we were to the constant issue of every kind of thing an earnest War Office can stick or hang on the infantryman. Everything but food, and not a scrap could be found with the most careful search.

As our left had halted, or were held up, it was decided to form a line of defense; evening was not far off and our right flank was in the air. A good road made this comparatively easy and there came the first chance of a rest.

A room roughly cleared as a Headquarters; the wounded were given water, but we could do nothing else and just let them lie. Their moaning was pitiful; some of them were dead. One man sang little songs in his delirium, and cried a name at intervals; we thought it must be his wife, as a photograph of a woman and some children lay on his breast. It was miserable to hear him crying for someone to help his loneliness and pain; when he died it was a great relief. The shell that did the damage brought one very curious sight; An engineer, up a telegraph pole, had been instantly beheaded; by some instinct he had clasped the pole and slid to the foot in that moment of death. There he knelt, without his head, still clasping the pole.

With the rest, my knee began to give trouble and swelled rapidly; in a short time the leg was useless. The discomfort of that night will remain as an outstanding war memory. A savage frost stiffened our clothes, for the house would be a trap in case of a counter attack and we lay in the open ditch. It took a philosophical mind to review the situation, with no right flank, no food, little ammunition, and the prospect of a counter attack. But nothing happened; beyond a few shots and an occasional flare the enemy gave no sign; in the general misery an attack would have been welcomed and met with the bayonet. Towards daybreak biscuits and rum arrived, with news that the flank was patched and victory complete and certain. Next morning fresh troops passed through us to the attack; the forcing of the Piave was accomplished.

A bugle hangs on a wall in Scotland, a bugle that once rang to the 38th Austrian Regiment, whose badge was a silver miniature of the steel 'Dolly Varden' Queer the moves of Fate. But the bugle inspired these memories, and a thousand others of Asiago, and the Alps, and the Plaines, and old world towns of Northern Italy. The snows and pine clad mountains weave their pictures with the men that passed or lived, the weary marches, the happy days in camp or town.

But one memory is clear above all; that daybreak on Piave when the 'Gordon's' burst through the brushwood to the white shingle. Veiled in blue haze, the evil yellow flash of shrapnel above, the black river in front, the rattle of machine guns to tear the still morning silence.

Men crashing from the wood, men running over the shingle, men splashing through the stream, men struggling through the wire.

Shouts and yells, with the savage gleam of the bayonet and the spurt of rifle fire, the sprawling collapse on the shingle, the floundering of the hit in the swift running river. What a scene for an artist; and yet, who could show the virile life, the savage determination of the assault, the wonderous thrill of fighting men in action!

But the passing years dim memories; only the Austrian bugle remains, hung on a wall in Scotland, to bring again the memory of that autumn morning and the forcing of the River Piave.

****

Tributes & Obituaries

Late Major W.N. Brown
A Tribute

'When Earl Cavan, commanding the troops on the Italian front, made his final attack against the Austrian's in October, 1918, we were withdrawn from the Asiago Plateau, in the alps and rushed through Treviso onto the River Piave. We crossed on to the island of Papadopoli which formed part of the Delta of the river and was held by the Austrians. On the 22nd October, a storm broke over the area, the river was deluged for about five days, it was impossible to get reinforcements, and we were all marooned. On the morning of the 27th the weather cleared and the sound of the pipes – music to the ears – could be heard, much to our relief, and who should arrive on the island but Major W.N.Brown, ("Buster" Brown as he was affectionately known in the regiment) with a company of the 2nd Gordons. It was not long before they had the island cleared, and the prisoners taken. They continued the attack across the river along the main road to the town of Sachelli which they captured, and then onto the town of Pordenonni where the Austrians surrendered on the 5th November, 1918, to the shouts of "Armistecio – de Guerra fineto," from the populace. With the 2nd Gordons under the command of Major Brown victory in this sector was assured.'
J.J.F

****

Mr W Neilson Brown
Death of Well-known Border Man
Border Telegraph, September 1953

The death occurred in Peel Hospital on Monday of Mr William Neilson Brown, the only son of the late Mr A.L. Brown, who was at one time Liberal M.P. for the Border Burghs.
Mr Brown was born in Galashiels in 1883 and was educated at St Mary's, Melrose, and Eastbourne College. He joined his father in the tweed manufacturing firm of Brown Brothers, Buckholm Mill, an association which ended in 1927.

Before the first World War, Mr Brown was a member of the Border Rifle Volunteers and was known as a very fine shot. He competed frequently at Bisley where he won several prizes.
During the first World War he served in France and Italy with the 2nd Battalion, The Gordon Highlanders, and gained the Military Cross. He reached the rank of Major.
In the last war he was engaged in the censorship division of the Admiralty and was stationed at Scapa Flow. Later he was on the staff of I.C.I. St Boswells.
Mr Brown had a wide knowledge of the Borders and he wrote many interesting articles, many of which appeared in the columns of 'The Weekly Scotsman'. He

retained his keenness for rifle shooting and among his hobbies were fishing and gardening.
He leaves a widow and one son and one daughter.

****

Notable Borderer
Soldier and Writer
Southern Reporter, September 1953

His many Border friends heard with regret of the death at Peel Hospital of Mr William Neilson Brown, who was well known in Galashiels, Melrose, Selkirk and Ettrick.

The only son of the late Mr A.L. Brown, former Liberal M.P. for the Border Burghs, he was born in Galashiels in 1883, and was educated at St Mary's School, Melrose and Eastbourne College. He was associated with his father in the firm of Brown Brothers, Buckholm Mill until 1927.

Mr Brown was a member of the Border Rifle Volunteers and won several prizes at Bisley. During the first World War he served in France and Italy with the 2nd Battalion, The Gordon Highlanders, and gained the Military Cross. He attained the rank of Major.

In the last war he was engaged in the censorship division of the Admiralty at Scapa Flow. Later with I.C.I. at St Boswells.

Allied to a remarkable knowledge of the Borders, was a gift for descriptive writing. Many of his articles appeared in 'The Southern Annual' and other well known magazines. He was the author if a novel, a powerful story with a Border setting. He retained his keenness for rifle shooting, and was fond of fishing and gardening.

Mr Brown was cultured and kindly, and a true lover of literature and the beauties of the Borderland. Sympathy is extended to his wife, who is a daughter of Mrs MacGowan, Fairholm, Ettrickbridge, and to his son and daughter. The son who holds an important post in Kashmir had a distinguished military career in the last war.

****

Higher Commander's Remarks

'A fine leader of men, cheerful under all circumstances and very popular with all ranks. This officer gave up a temporary majority in the R.A.S.C. to become a Lieutenant in the Gordon Highlanders during the fighting on the Somme 1916.'
H.R. Green, Brigadier General, Commanding, 20th Infantry Brigade

****

Bugle taken from a trumpeter at the Austrian brigade
headquarters, during the battle of Piave.

The bugle now hangs on display in the Gordon Highland
Museum, Aberdeen.

Gordon Highlanders Museum

****

As well as the Bugle there is also a scrapbook filled with maps, postcards, photos and other memorabilia that William Brown compiled. Although, not on public display, due to its delicacy, you can still view it on request.

****

Special thanks to Jesper Ericsson, Curator at the Gordon Highlanders Museum, Aberdeen and to all the staff for their amazing work and time dedicated to the Gordon Highlanders Museum.

****

The Gordon Highlanders Museum
St. Luke's, Viewfield Road, Aberdeen, AB15 7XH
Tel: 01224 311200 | Fax: 01224 319323
www.gordonhighlanders.com

The Gordon Highlanders Museum is an independent self-financed museum, governed by a charitable trust. Registered Charity No. SCO22039

****

10% from the sale of this book shall be donated to the Gordon Highlanders Museum.

****

To purchase more copies please visit: www.allwellyet.co.uk

****

'All Well Yet' - compiled by Timothy James Brown – Grandson of William Neilson Brown

****

Made in the USA
Charleston, SC
27 July 2014